BEYOND THE WALLS

Beyond the Walls
New Writing from York St John University

2018

Valley Press

First published in 2018 by Valley Press
Woodend, The Crescent, Scarborough, YO11 2PW
www.valleypressuk.com

ISBN 978-1-912436-08-8
Cat. no. VP0128

YORK CENTRE
FOR WRITING

Editorial content © York Centre for Writing 2018
Cover artwork © Hannah Ford 2018   Foreword © Naomi Booth 2018
Contents, pp11-128 © the indivdiual contributors, as credited 2018

'The Museum of Gilead Audio Transcript' (pp 19-23) is intended as a creative parody, which utilises characters and situations from *The Handmaid's Tale* (Margaret Atwood, 1985), as permitted by Section 30A of the Copyright, Designs and Patents Act 1988 (as amended in 2014).

A CIP record for this book is available from the British Library.

Text design by Jamie McGarry.

Printed and bound in Great Britain by Imprint Digital, Upton Pyne, Exeter.

Contents

Foreword   *Dr Naomi Booth*   7
Preface   *Student Editorial Team*   9

Paris in the Rain   *Charlotte Brindley*   11
How's Uni Going?   *Jacob Brown*   14
Mayfly   *Zoe Buckton*   16
The Museum of Gilead Audio Transcript   *Tia Byer*   19
Cheat on Me   *Revie Byrnes*   24
The Stillness of Time   *Rachel Colley*   25
Strings   *Emma Collier*   28
But I Guess Some Things Are Better Left Unsaid   *Tash Curry*   29
Corky's Children   *Georgia Cuthbertson*   30
Wolf by Wolf   *Lauren Davies*   31
Laundry Room   *Katie Dicks*   35
The Cell   *Alex Eglen*   38
Voice   *Elizabeth Fitzgerald*   41
Yours, Lucy   *Gabriella Gadaleta*   42
My Pal – In Memoriam   *Robin Gallagher*   44
Human Atrocity   *Natalie Gardner*   46
I Am   *Claire Hagan*   48
The Cage   *Rachel Hancock*   49
Who You Are Today   *Hannah Herraghty*   52
Dressed in Black   *BethenyJo*   55
Art Gallery   *Elliott Hurst*   57
He Could Sense Death Coming and Still Rose Up   *Anna Jeffries*   58
Some Day Soon   *Daniel Johnson*   60
In Sanity   *R. E. Kirby*   61
Be There by Ten   *Abby Knowles*   62
Parched   *Abby Knowles*   63
The Mosquito in My Chardonnay   *Kelsey Leigh*   64
Drowned by a Copper Sea   *Heather Lukins*   66
Problem of the Nature of Man   *Heather Lukins*   70
Sentinel   *Hugh McCormick*   71

Cupid Painted Blind   *Rachel McHale*   74
Greece 1991   *Emma McKenzie*   77
Cailleach   *Emma McNicholas*   80
Reaper   *Rupert Nevin*   82
Vitality   *B. T. Oldfield*   84
Elisa Day   *Mathew Payne*   85
The Lost Legions   *Nicoletta Peddis*   86
I Counted to Eleven   *Matthew Pickering*   89
Blackout   *Elisabeth Prestgard*   92
Chaos in the Improv   *Laura Russell*   94
Stays time   *Laura Russell*   95
1947   *Kathryn Sharman*   96
Signs of Rain   *Benjamin Shaw*   98
October 11th 1988   *Joe Shaw*   99
ignorance equals fear equals silence equals death   *Joe Shaw*   100
He Who Stole Me Away   *Megan Shield*   102
The Giant's Gold   *A. L. Smith*   104
Days of the Week   *Emily Smith*   107
The Noise They Make   *Rachel Smith*   108
Unkindness   *Samuel Stanford*   110
Snowkissed   *Gemma Strydom*   113
The Seal Woman   *Megan Tait-Davies*   115
The Swan   *E. L. Thompson*   117
The Flowers That Frighten Me   *Holly Whitford*   120
The Midnight Ride with the Púca   *Jess Whittall*   122
The Recorder   *Scott Winsbury*   123
Waiting   *David Yeomans*   126
Bloodjack   *Tom Young*   127

Acknowledgements   129

Foreword

When we first named our student anthology *Beyond the Walls*, we couldn't have predicted how walls, and the divisions they create, would become such pressing concerns in the following years. Plans for new walls, for newly-enforced borders, and for new boundaries seem to be under constant construction just now. But writers have always treated walls with contempt and suspicion: good writing is often mole-work, tunneling under the ramparts of the past and coming up in new places; sometimes it's a straightforward demolition job. The title of this anthology seems newly resonant this year, in terms of the importance of the task of writing with an outward focus.

In Kafka's famous parable 'Before the Law', a man arrives at a gate in a wall, seeking admission. The gatekeeper tells him that entry may be possible, but not now. The man waits. The man waits so long that he grows old, and bent, and blind. He has little time left to live, but still he waits, until 'he recognizes now in the darkness an illumination which breaks inextinguishably out of the gateway'. Seeing that the man is dying, the gatekeeper finally closes the door against him. Kafka's brutal tale of waiting and insurmountable barriers reminds me that as writers we pursue that inextinguishable 'illumination', even when the gates seem liable to close against us. All of the writers included here are doing just that: striving to connect to something and someone beyond the barriers of themselves in the act of writing and being published. It's strenuous and demanding work, and there are many barriers to doing it. We're immensely proud of all the student work included here and of the years of hard work and tenacity represented in these pieces.

When we're teaching Creative Writing, we often talk about literary gatekeepers: those powerful individuals who control access to the world of publishing, be they agents, or editors, or reviewers. In recent years there's been a surge of challenges to the way the literary world is policed, to the border control of literary culture. New publishers are focussing on work by writers who have been excluded in the past, and on new ways of getting work to readers. Our second-year students working on our Production, Publication and Performance module have been immersed in thinking about this over the last semester, and it's their work that has brought this anthology into being, alongside the indefatigable efforts of Dr Kimberly Campanello and our new publishing partner, Valley Press. Our students have tirelessly read and edited and promoted the work of the other students included here, as well as selecting cover art from among the immensely talented artists and designers at YSJU, and they've organised a launch and showcase event. They're our gate-openers of the future; they're already helping to shape a big, bright illuminated world of writing that is beyond walls.

As our students have been putting the finishing touches to this anthology, York has been held fast in snow, big fat flakes settling on the Minster and the pavements and the famous city walls. Our youngest students sometimes have to deal with the accusation from the popular press that they are a generation of 'snowflakes'; especially fragile and friable. The work collected here is a reminder of the total fallacy of this charge: our young people face intense pressures and the Creative Writers at YSJU illuminate some of these struggles for us. One definition of compassion is a turning towards suffering: and this is what our writers do, never flinching away from difficult things, practising compassion on the page. The work collected here engages with environmental crisis, with war, with the suffering of animals, with grief and repression and discrimination. There are creation stories here, and stories of extinctions. There are poems about the wild pleasures of our bodies and about their dangers. There are tales about murder and illness and suicide and transformation and hope. And all of this is managed with wit and invention and emotional heft. I've watched the snowflakes turn to compacted ice in York over the last few days, full of glitter and brilliance, and I've thought of this bright, brilliant writing.

Many of our students included here are also involved in speculating on the future: they write about fantastical new worlds. But all writing is to some extent an act of the future: it holds out a promise for the reader of something new. With this anthology, we celebrate the achievements of this cohort of Creative Writing graduates, and of their determination and energy in creating the future. In the words of one of the writers and demolition experts included in this book, Tom Young, we hope that after graduation they continue to write and to live, 'As if life was a pipe running under the Earth / And we burst it'.

Dr Naomi Booth
Subject Director for Creative Writing
March 2018

Preface

North of the historical walls of York lies York St John University; a fountain of creative intent fuelled by the minds of our talented students. Each word is a stone as old as the Roman foundations, enriched with Viking lore and Tudor architecture. York is a centrepiece of history and our students have taken this past, weaving and sewing it into our future. We have witnessed the construction of this anthology as York has seen the rise of empires – now it falls to you.

Discover the future written in the prose and poetry ahead; explore, enjoy and let us take you on a journey through the works forged *Beyond the Walls*.

Student Editorial Team
March 2018

Paris in the Rain

I watch as the last sugar cube floating on top of Nora's latte finally sinks into the rich brown depths below.

'So how's your new boss?' Nora asks, stirring her drink.

I'm halfway through eating a mouthful of brownie. I wave my hand nonchalantly. 'He's an arse. He refuses to call me Genie, shrieking Genevieve down the corridor. I hate it.'

I look out the window. It's raining. The streets are empty, for now. York's pretty quiet during a Friday afternoon: everyone is still at work or preparing for the school run. When it hits three o'clock, people will swarm from all corners of the city. Then we'll see him.

'Probably because he's not used to human company,' Nora replies.

I nod. 'It's early days, he'll get used to me soon. How many android devices have your company acquired since I last saw you?'

Nora groans. 'Fifteen and fuck me they're annoying. So compliant and boring! It's like talking to a brick wall. I haven't had a good bitch in days!' she whines.

We both laugh. The waiter approaches us. He doesn't say anything, he just smiles and collects the wrapper from Nora's biscuits and the used napkins. His eyes are electric green. I say a gentle thank you as he works.

Nora ignores him, she moves closer to the window away from him. 'I swear, they're everywhere nowadays, it's getting harder and harder to determine who's what,' she scoffs.

The news pops up on the TV. The date and the time flash briefly before the newsreader appears in his shiny blue suit. It's the 10th of August 2154. The time is 2:59pm. I look at Nora anxiously.

'Relax Genie, he'll be here.' Nora smirks.

The waiter walks away from our table. I spot the microchip bolted to the back of his neck.

The giant clock outside strikes three. I ask Nora about her newest date to occupy the time. I joke about her knowing if he really is human, and I'm punished with the finite detail of the gross oozing wound on his leg from a rugby accident, and the size and description of his genitalia. I check my watch, it's four minutes past three.

There he is. Like clockwork. He appears from behind the bank and strides across the pavement. My face must be glowing because Nora throws a sugar packet at me.

'He's here.' I smile.

Nora laughs. 'Let's have a look at him today.'

Oh my God, he is so dreamy. Flawless skin; his lean, toned body wrapped in a dark grey suit. Messy black curls decorate his perfect head, they are slicked back today showing more of his beautiful face.

I lean against the window, watching the rain droplets trickle down like I'm in some sort of music video. 'Isn't he just dreamy?' I ask. 'He's like hot chocolate by a roaring fire.'

'Like cocktails on a beach,' Nora adds. 'Fireworks and champagne.'

'Like Paris in the rain.'

Nora and I both laugh. We watch him enter the coffee shop, our coffee shop. He's at the counter ordering his espresso, like he does every Friday at exactly 3:11pm, like clockwork. Nora and I hide behind our seats, but occasionally peep over the top to see him.

'Why don't you go and talk to him?' Nora asks suddenly.

'You're crazy,' I scoff.

Nora launches forward in her chair, capturing my hands in her own. The coffee on the table forgotten.

'Go and talk to him!' she demands.

'No, I couldn't!' I immediately retort.

'Genie, he could be the one, your one! Your Paris in the rain with fireworks and champagne and roses. The worst he can say is no.'

'Or he says that he's married. I'd look like a total fool.'

Nora pinches the skin on my palms. 'Your boss makes you look a fool every day, why don't you go and let someone attractive do it for once?'

I laugh, but Nora has a point. I have no idea why, but I stand and start to walk to the counter.

As I walk, I can feel sweat pooling in my palms. My heart is racing and I'm finding it hard to swallow. I'm a mess, and I haven't even spoken to him yet. I'm panicking. I can't just approach him, I need something to say. Think, Genie! Something clever.

I stumble up to the counter, the waiter from earlier is there. He cocks his head.

'Can I help you miss?' He asks.

'Ermm.' I pause, physically shaking when I notice the attractive man's eyes are on me. 'Erm yes, I'm not feeling too good, can I have a glass of water?'

The waiter nods. 'Yes, of course, miss. I will be right back.'

He disappears.

I wait. Now what? I feel a hand on my shoulder. Oh God.

'Excuse me, I heard you are unwell, can I help?'

I turn. It's him. Fuck me, it's him. I can't breathe.

He smiles. 'I am not a doctor, but I do have first aid training so I can offer some assistance.' He walks to an empty table and pulls out a chair. 'Please, sit.'

I sit.

He sits opposite and presses a hand against my forehead. 'You do feel very warm. I do not think you have a temperature though.'

The waiter appears again and places the glass down beside me. I smile as he nods and walks off again. I snatch the glass and start slurping it down.

I breathe. 'I'm okay, I just felt a bit light headed, maybe I'm just dehydrated,' I lie. I rub my sweaty hand against my leg before I offer it him, I watch my own fingers tremble. 'I'm Genie.'

He smiles. 'Archie,' he takes my hand and shakes it.

'I'm going to blame it on me feeling ill, but I don't suppose you would like to grab a drink sometime?' I blurt out.

His face contorts and I bury my head in my hand. 'I'm so sorry, you've got a girlfriend, or a boyfriend! I'm so sorry, it's honestly okay! I'm sorry!' I sob.

Archie laughs. 'No no, I am single!' He laughs. 'It is just that I did not expect you to ask me! I have noticed you every time I come here and I have wanted to talk to you, but you are always with your friend and I get nervous.'

I can't believe it. My heart sky rockets, I don't think it's even in my chest anymore! A smile slaps my face into motion. 'Really?'

Archie nods. 'I must dash off, but shall we meet here again tomorrow morning? Say around eleven? I will take you out for lunch and we can get to know each other a bit more?'

My face reddens. 'I'd love that!'

'See you tomorrow then, Genie,' Archie smiles and gets up to leave. His eyes are gorgeous: electric green in colour.

He gives me a wave before he turns and leaves the coffee shop. As he opens the door, the wind catches his hair and lifts it around his ears.

There's a microchip on the nape of his neck.

Charlotte Brindley

How's Uni Going?

How's Uni going?
I'm fine
Never been better actually
All clinical, by the book, factual
Fucking hate it really but yeah
There ya go
University
You don't know me
Make it a hot drink to go
Tip toe and slide away
Before this jar topples and falls
Messy clean up
Intended break up
This'll take more than a patch up
Sellotape on open wounds
Laughing through the bad
Just to scrape a bit of luck
Never been one for looks
Doesn't stop mum
From buttering it up
Clueless
She'd be better off keeping her mouth shut
Sometimes you've gotta dig deep
When you're in a rut
Always the butt
Had enough of all the bullshit
They're kicking up
Motors like a train
To evade all the topics
That are puzzling the brain
What next?
Search in vain but
You don't get answers
From throwing it at Google

Stubbed in strudel
She's wearing nowt but strawberry laces
Little bit crude but still
I'm just a curious lad
Yanno it's all about the nudes still
Student inbuilt
Scrambling enough cash
Just to get a pot noodle
Little bit rude still
Escaping 9-5 and H_2O bills
Nah there's no easy street
Or Jack's magic fucking beans
You can hide by all means
But you can't runaway
Speaks volumes of the industry
She's just not that into me
Clearly
It's my responsibility
To mind for head injuries
When getting my hands dirty
In strawberry fields
Plucking from the apple tree

Jacob Brown

Mayfly

Her contractions are hot and spiky. They remind Sophie of something she saw at a history exhibition, something on the boxes everyone had – static. She remembers thinking it was shit, her memory skewed by her organs being tugged at, feeling every sensation through a thick layer of sweat. The rain is merciless. She closes her eyes and tries to relax her muscles, picturing Milo's first breaths somewhere else. Somewhere with clean air. She can't picture it for long, the pain returns, plunging her into delirium. She glances through the archway of the bedroom to the front door.

I can make it.

She gathers her breath, and whistles for her housedroid. Gripping the bedsheets, she slides onto the floor. She lies sideways on the cool marble, under the housedroid's harsh, blue guidelight. Nausea courses through her. She wonders if it's labour or revulsion at the fear of emptying. Pouring her body out into a city of streetshovels built for feathers and flesh.

Dan snores in the office. He'd slept through the owls. Even the eagles. He'd wanted to be involved in every part of the birth, but had refused to let her look outside during the rain. She still feels bitter. She pushes through the archway on her side, protecting the curve of her belly with a soaking wet support pillow. The housedroid follows her slowly. It normally zipped around, washing the red stains from the doormat, making toast. Its slow crawl seems sarcastic, like the little bot is mocking her. She looks it dead in the lightbulbs.

I can UN-invent you, y'know.

It scuttles off leaving her slumped against the front door. She wonders whether she can thrust her arm up without passing out, and tries. As she swings her hand she realises she can't recognise it. Her fingers are a blur, multiplying. She can barely grasp the handle. The metal is cold, the shock reunites her with the sensations of her skin. She clamps her hand down with all the force she can muster. The rest of her body joins in, forming the most brutal contraction yet. She closes her eyes and lowers her head onto the pavement outside. The taste of metal makes her teeth hurt. She breathes in, splutters, and opens her eyes to find that the ground is moving.

Thousands of black legs, striped yellow bellies and brown abdomens are tipped towards the mauve sky. The noise is primal. Droning. Sophie strains her eyes. Their wings are warped and twisted. Their antennae and furry legs thick with digidust. She bends her legs and pushes herself out through the door. She groans with the effort. Bees crawl over her arms, her legs. Five of them fall from the sky onto her bump. She remembers her mother, who told her these little things are the sentinels of the earth. Now they lie ready to be scraped up by the droids tomorrow morning. Her muscles spasm, her jaw wavers. She can't stop herself from letting out a scream. She writhes with the creatures, and they writhe with her. The bees fall from the night, and bury her. She sees Dan peering over them, his dark skin swathed in moonlight, his eyes wide, his teeth showing. He is screaming too.

*

She wakes up in a tilted bed, holding her still and upright. She turns her head and the walls lag behind. Her skin is slimy and warm. She can feel a sharp sting between her legs. She longs to move her ankles, but finds they're strapped down. She blinks. She needs to be sick. As she wretches a medidroid detaches a bowl from the top of its unit, as if tipping a hat.

'Get it all out,' says a supervisory doctor from the corner, surrounded in tobacco vapour.

'Where is my daughter?' Sophie says. She wretches again.

'In the watchtanks,' says the doctor.

Sophie blinks. She wants to ask what has happened. She struggles to lean forward. The doctor crosses the room towards Sophie and wordlessly pushes her back with a gloved hand. She begins to negotiate the tubes feeding into Sophie's arm.

At the watchtanks, Dan stands over his daughter. Her fingernails are tiny. Her eyes are huge. Her few strands of hair are tightly coiled. She stares at him through the incubation unit. He stares back, puzzled. He rubs his arm, it is bandaged loosely. it took doctors hours to remove all the stingers whilst his wife gave birth three wards away. Dan thinks of Sophie lying there, naked, the bugs crawling everywhere. Her chest. Her neck. He rubs at the blotches on his hands. He is glad the bees are gone. The nurse arrives.

'She was dipping in and out of consciousness, she has no stings. You can see her now.'

Dan follows the droid and the incubation chamber as they float down a red, illuminated track. They reach the sanitation ward. The incubation unit lowers gently. Dan pushes through the curtain. Sophie is sprawled on her back, sweaty. He steers the incubation unit towards her. She smiles, reaches out to the glass with her forefinger. She wipes her eyes, presses a button on her bedside. There is a clicking sound, blue liquid trails towards her wrist in a long translucent tube.

'Can I hold her?'

'Not yet,' says Dan. 'They have to check her.'

'For what? She looks fine!' She blows air into her cheeks, Milo pouts.

'For contamination. You were out there, with those… things.'

'Bees?' she says, 'There's nothing wrong with them.'

'Really?' says Dan. He pulls down the bandages on his arm. Sophie examines the stings. 'Well you need dock leaf for that. Or was it nettles. I don't remember. If you're nice to them, they're nice to you.'

Dan grimaces, Sophie breathes deeply and reaches down beneath her legs. She can feel stitches holding her together, rough edges. She winces.

A projection unit starts up without warning in the cubicle. A smiling woman stands in the centre of the image. The ward becomes silent.

'The rains are over. We can announce the final toll.' The list fills the room. 'Wood Pigeon, Collared Dove, Damselfly, Pipistrelle Bat, Starling.'

Sophie fiddles with the plastic seal on the incubation unit and pulls Milo out, holding her to her chest.

'Bumblebee, Kingfisher, Nuthatch. Seagull, Raven, Snowy Owl, Tawny Owl, Pink-Footed Goose.'

A nurse alerted to the broken containment seal runs into the room. He sees the newscaster and stands in shock.

'Lesser Horseshoe Bat, Sparrow, Goldfinch, Carpenter Bee, Chrysomya, Barnacle Goose, Yellowhammer.'

The nurse looks out of the window. The streets are empty. The rooftops are empty. There is nothing. The list goes on for hours. Dan looks at Sophie. Sophie looks at Milo. Milo looks at the sky, where the maintenance droids shine like fireflies.

Zoe Buckton

The Museum of Gilead Audio Transcript

Welcome to the Museum of Gilead. I will be your audio tour guide, Dalton Moonrise.

Found in the heart of the Republic of Massachusetts, this time capsule offers a comprehensive look at the notorious regime, as well as the oppressive behavioural controls it enforced upon its female citizens.

The Museum of Gilead was founded by the Historical Preservation Society, here at the district of Cambridge's University of Veritas.

Located within the university's ancient walls, this museum is home to the oldest campus to pre-date the Gileadean era.

Gilead transformed America into a regimented patriarchal state of tyranny. Social and sexual activities were controlled and biblical ideologies enforced. This led to the suppression of the majority of the population, particularly women.

In response to the decline of birth rates during the late 1980s, the government introduced the New Rights family values. This criminalised practices that interfered with sexual reproduction. Such practices included abortion, homosexuality and religious vows of celibacy.

It is estimated that approximately 11 million people were killed under the Gileadean rule. The Republic fell after the allied forces of England and Canada invaded during the 2099 revolution.

Today the Museum of Gilead offers a chilling insight into the brutal history of Gilead.

To learn about each exhibition individually, press the relevant letter displayed by each information point on your auditory info pad.

To listen to the first exhibit, press A.

You are now in the Rachel and Leah Re-education Centre exhibition.

If you have come at a busy time, you may have to queue to get a closer look at each item. In the meantime, we can learn about this state-orchestrated programme where Handmaids were trained.

The makeshift prison camp was once the college gymnasium here, at the previously known Harvard University.

Also called the Red Centre by its inhabitants, the Rachel and Leah Re-education Centre is where unmarried fertile women were drugged and brought by force.

Exhibit A is a photograph taken by the allied forces during the revolution. It shows the liberation of the centre.

Notice how the sign above the building is painted in a deep red colour.

The colour and the name symbolise the sexuality of the Handmaid's duty. The name of the centre is derived from the book of Genesis in the Bible.

Rachel and Leah were sisters who both became wives of Jacob. Each sister gave their handmaid to Jacob so he could produce children.

Therefore, a Handmaid's role as the breeder of the next generation was justified by Biblical precedent.

Exhibit 2 is an example of one of the brainwashing programmes the centre authorized. This film presents a biased survey of sexual politics from the 1970s and 1980s.

The film shows clips from feminist rallies about pro-abortion and anti-pornography. This propaganda demonstrates how Gilead believed that their enforced social order could offer women 'freedom from' male violence, by providing them with the 'freedom to' live in a respectful and safer world.

Exhibit 3 displays the contemporary artist Xenia Hawthorne's painting 'The Kingdom of God'.

Based on the accounts of real handmaids, this painting depicts the explicit association between women and breeding animals. It is set within the Rachel and Leah Re-education Centre. This painting shows the handmaids being guarded by Aunts holding live electric cattle prods.

The ghost-like figures in black represent the Angel soldiers of Gilead. These soldiers guarded the inhabitants of Gilead.

Look at the crying Handmaid. She is dressed in her white training uniform. How do you think she is feeling?

When you are ready to move onto the next exhibition, press B.

The Handmaid exhibition.

You are now entering our Handmaid exhibition.

On the right, we have Exhibit 4, the handmaid's uniform.

A red dress and white headpiece were issued to each handmaid upon arrival at the Centre. The uniform's conservative design was derived from the biblical teaching of Timothy. According to the Bible, 'women should dress modestly'.

Look closer at the mannequin's hand.

Notice the tattooed four-digit number?

Each Handmaid was issued a number. Her former name was replaced with her master's name. This new form of identity was intended to symbolise her status as his slave.

In Gilead, women were reduced to passivity. A woman was a sexual commodity whose only purpose was producing offspring for the state.

Exhibit 5 shows us a reconstructed bedroom typical of a commander's house.

As a surrogate to the household, the most important event in a Handmaid's posting was the impregnation ceremony.

Perhaps the bleakest aspect of the Gileadean era, this state-sanctioned rape took place once a month when the Handmaid was at her most fertile.

The ceremony consisted of the Commander, the Commander's Wife and the Handmaid all participating in sexual activity. If a Handmaid did not conceive after several months, she would be reassigned to another posting. Continued failure resulted in being sent to the colonies, where she would be classed as an unwoman.

To see our birthing exhibition, continue into the next room and press C on your info pad.

Birthing Exhibition.

We are now looking at Exhibit 6, a birthing stool.

The most significant event in the Gileadean calendar was the birth of a child. Gilead dictated that all births should take place at home and in the presence of an all-female audience.

Attended by neighbouring wives and handmaids, a birth day was a compulsory outing. Gilead's emphasis on the importance of natural childbirth embraced the idea that painful childbirth was the just punishment for Eve's original sin. No pain relief was used during the birth.

Now imagine what it was like during the birth of a child. Imagine the heat, smell of blood and sweat. Imagine the Handmaid giving her baby to the wife, now that her one purpose has been executed. Would she feel sadness, or would she be relived?

Exhibit 7 displays the shredder.

This machine was devised by the state to shred disabled babies.

Gilead was obsessed with perfection. The smallest 'mutation' could classify a newborn as an 'unbaby'. Birth deformities had increased prior to the inception of Gilead. Environmental pollution and natural disasters meant that the birth rate had plummeted.

It is unknown exactly how many babies were murdered.

Look at the blood-stained hydraulic metal sheers. It is estimated that this killing machine would take just under a second to slaughter an unbaby.

To move onto the final exhibition press D.

The Handmaid's Tale Exhibition.

We are now in our final exhibit.

Exhibit 8 features the original tapes containing the infamous story of 'The Handmaid's Tale'.

These tapes were found in the ruins of the city of Bangor, Maine. They were discovered, hidden in an army footlocker.

The published transcript was then edited by two professors at the University of Cambridge.

Look closely at the labels of the tapes. The music dates back almost 250 years.

Although the original identity of the narrator 'Offred' is unknown, it is believed that she was among the first wave of Handmaids.

Offred's fate is also unknown. However, many historians believe she was one of the lucky few to escape to either Canada or England.

I hope you have enjoyed your tour. Goodbye.

Tia Byer
(after Margaret Atwood)

Cheat on Me

Drunk slurs of advancements,
wet kisses of deceit.
'I've got a –'
Tongues encourage silence,
intimate heat.
'We can't –'
Search for protection,
shame-stained sheets.

Trophy of indignity,
printed on your neck.
'You okay?'
Heartbeat pulsing,
concerned texts.
'I'm ok.'
Conceal the truth,
of hidden sex.

Revie Byrnes

The Stillness of Time

I can feel the severe pain coursing through my joints as I sit on a cold, hard steel chair

I glance around to ignore the pain and see my Mum looking straight ahead I don't know why she's not communicating with me maybe it's because she already knows why we're here and doesn't want me to panic

too late for that now I'm on the verge of having a breakdown I should be able to control my panic attack like I did last night

it's so hard to disguise the feeling of panic rising in my throat I don't want to make a scene in the middle of the surgery I want to just be able to get through this appointment and get out of here

as I contemplate on trying to remain calm I hear some noisy kids coming around the corner of the hallway to the waiting room great more noise

I try and ignore the loud screeches and voices and focus on my hands while I try and control the panic in my throat that is threatening to cover my whole body the sound of my name 'Miss Williams' coming from the nurse who magically appears at the corner of my vision fills me with relief as I get up quickly from the chair to escape the now chaotically loud waiting room

the office is light and airy the room is a pale blue it seemed that all hospital rooms had to be that colour or a sickly green and I can hear rushing cars outside letting me know that the morning traffic was well underway

now what can I do for you Miss Williams

the nurse looks at me expectantly and I feel myself become more nervous under her stern gaze and turn to face my Mum

my Mum doesn't respond to the question and I realise she's wanting me to answer I'm so used to not having to talk with the Doctor much

I think I may have a consultant who is doing the treatment that you need that I can refer you to him if you want me to

I look to my Mum again and thankfully this time she decides to help me out my head is whirring with all the dates that I have booked and my head starts to ache with all the information I don't feel relief from the situation until yes that would be great wouldn't it Lyra

yes that be great really I definitely need this treatment and if this is the best consultant for the job then I'm sure nothing will go wrong

from the chuckling sound coming from the Doctor I can tell I've been caught out with my not listening to the conversation I just can't help it when my Mum and the Doctor are talking about things I don't understand or care about my mind just wanders

well I can't promise anything but he is one of the best consultants for this kind of treatment and I wouldn't have recommended him if I hadn't of thought so

I nod in a robotic fashion and can feel my muscles tense around my mouth as I offer him a fake smile and say

well I'm just glad something can be done about this pain it's starting to distract me from my University life and I hate it when my health is keeping me from doing anything

the doctor nods and his head starts to become a blur with how tired my eyes feel

education is something that we take seriously here at the surgery and if we can we will make sure we can fit this treatment around your study it will be hard though because of all the government cuts so we are limited with what we can do but we'll try everything we can

I nod and my neck seems not to be working properly if I can't get out of this room I feel as if my body will seize up if I don't get out

thanks again for everything

is there anything more I can do for you today

just as a recap so I know you know all of this but I'll refer you Lyra to this consultant and you can book an appointment with him nearer the time my joints are groaning and my mind feels as if its groaning along with it with how slow this appointment is taking

thank you

when the door opens back into the real world the noise of the people shocks my senses slightly

well that went more smoothly than I thought it would do what do you think about it all Lyra

why can't people just leave me alone in peace for a few seconds everyone seems to want to know my take on things

I think it's great mum I can't wait to meet this consultant he must be good if the doctor thinks so highly of him

getting out of the building was something of a relief that building always seemed to get too stuffy and the sunshine was forgiving and warmed my body up

you know I want the utmost happiness for you don't you Lyra

Lyra you do know that don't you

yes I know mum I'm fine I just want this appointment over and done with

I know I know darling and we'll get through this but you just have to get through this semester and you'll be pain free this summer

I know it's just that I want a summer you know and this operation won't allow me to have one

look I understand that you're frustrated about this situation but you've been through this before and I'm sure you'll do absolutely fine in this situation

the shake of my head makes me realise that I probably sound like a whiny bitch if I said all of this out loud and I resolve to make sure that no one hears of my self-deprecating thoughts other than myself I didn't need anyone else other than myself at exactly how weak I am I don't care if I'm putting on a face to people it's just what I do it's how I survive with this condition in this world

Rachel Colley

Strings

I
Tie
Myself up
Into neat bows
Fold myself in
To
Cocooned space.
And pray
In the dark
I look so neat on the outside
When I'm breaking in a space
They can't find.
I look at you
And
Accidently,
Stand on the cord that binds me
In.
I'm unravelled
Revealed.
Limp and lifeless

In your hands
Brown and worn
Hiding weeks,
Look closer, months,
Look closer, years,
All washed away by the tears
Of rain
And the bleach
That frayed
Soft skin
But now you look
At strangled string
The piece
That once was bow
You read my face,
That says,
I am a frayed.
You saw my bow
And thought me a gift
But I am sad strings
'fraid and careless worn.

Emma Collier

But I Guess Some Things Are Better Left Unsaid

There are unfinished stories lying in my room, they were our stories. Old pages just dying there, red ink seeping off the faded parchment, words, memories, history. Just disappearing. We were lost. Some stories never written, it was too hard. It hurt too much. Things I never got to say, written down. Letters I never sent. Answers I would never get. We fade with time, from words from forgotten memories we'd rather forget than keep. Those words I could never forget scarred into my memory, 'I would write about you, about us'. Somehow time forgot, we were lost in decaying pages. In the years to come I would remember us, how we were in the books I would write. The tragedy that we were. The tale we would become.

I always knew I would write our story, but I never thought it would be so difficult to write down the memories we had, the kisses we shared, the love we had. The lies we told, the promises we could never keep. The hearts that would soon be broken and the one that would never beat again. Our story was never an easy one; it was rushed, messy and too painful. I put myself through hell for you. I wrote the story I think we could have had, if our timing was different. Maybe in another universe, we end up together. Maybe in another life we were not just stories written among pages of lost love and tragic ends.

I wrote the story of how we died; did Shakespeare take you first just to spite me? There was no heaven or earth just the myth of fate. I know I will write about us, the way we met, the long full looks, the playful smiles, the forbidden kisses, our tragic downfall. The letter I wrote of our ever-dying love, the reply that never came. Our fate wasn't kind; we both knew that, we knew it would be difficult. We were against two different worlds, against ourselves. We were against the gods, the prophecy. As kids we were told our love could overcome anything. Our history would be repeated, it would be for centuries. We will be remembered as the lovers who overcame fate but at the cost of themselves.

I hope history will tell her I'm sorry for all the things I could not do, for all the things I never said – *but I guess some things are better left unsaid, but you were everything to me then.*

Tash Curry

Corky's Children

Male. Underfed. Ignored.
What is it? Mother shows uncertainty.
Trainers to step in. Feeding paramount to calf's survival.
In footnotes the word ~~force fed~~.
Age 18 days. Cause of death pneumonia and brain damage.

Two more calves. Repeated. Underfed. Ignored.
Incapable of mothering? No natural instincts.
Age equal to that of a child herself.
Trainers to train her to mother.
Age of death: 11 days. Cause of death: unknown.

Fourth calf female. Name: Kiva.
Positive outlook, wait. No, again, difficulties nursing.
Trainers take over feeding. Leads to aggressive play.
Separated from mother for calf's safety.
Age of death: 46 days. Cause of death: unknown.

No more notable live births.
Majority stillborn, miscarried.
Decision to be taken off the breeding programme.
Shows signs of surrogate mother tendencies.
Signed off by SeaWorld.
In footnotes ~~written off~~.

Georgia Cuthbertson

Wolf by Wolf

The wolf abandoned her den, driven by compulsion. She trekked east, pausing every few miles to mark her territory; she brushed against the rough bark of a poplar, its dark, sticky sap clung to pale fur in drops of amber.

A soft mewing cut through the racket of the woods and curled itself around the wolf's senses. Struggling to hear the sound over the bristling wind, she lifted her head, turning it to the side, pinpointing it. She stalked the noise; each cry came clearer and louder than the last.

And then, she saw it.

A small brown rabbit caught underneath a trapper's net.

The wolf resisted at first, despite the longing for the taste of rich juicy meat. She salivated at the thought of tearing through its pelt, snatching the warm goodness from its soft middle. She could take it by surprise. Chew into and break its thin flesh with her teeth.

Except she remained still, suspended between what she craved and the need to leave, to avoid temptation.

The rabbit fought against the trap, yanking and flipping its tiny body back and forth as it attempted to free itself.

She made her move then, slipping closer until she was leaning over it. The rabbit spasmed, releasing a shrill bleat. With her teeth, she latched her jaws around the rabbit.

Using her teeth, she pulled at the netting, catching fur in her mouth, and the earthy taste of rabbit on her tongue. She forced back the erupting huffs of breath erupting at the back of her throat.

Her sharp teeth snapped through the woven rope with tactile efficiency. The net split, and the rabbit was free. The wolf leapt away watching the rabbit buck, leap and run from her before she turned away, restless. Her pelt tingled under the breeze, the damp air electrified by the rising moon.

*

She swarmed the forest in a garnet cloak, the fabric seemingly black in the low light. She followed the river running east to west.

Hilde held the oil lamp up towards her face, the gold glow highlighting the sharp edges of her face, flush from the biting wind. She kept her hood down, sighing as the air licked at the skin of her neck and tugged playfully at her hair.

Heat pulsed beneath her skin, a living thing simmering on the precipice. It grew in strength the deeper she travelled through the woods. She took longer strides, stretching out the muscles in her legs in hopes of relieving the strain. This venture into the woods had been no choice of hers, or her twin's. She cursed the moon in silence, keeping her attention on the fall of her steps.

The gnarled branches hung above her, interloping towards the earth, reaching for her as she passed. She wiped a hand across her cheek, removing the silk caress of a web. The trees grew larger, the path lost to her some time ago. She went on, called forward by her memory. Behind her, the town lights flickered in the distance, their glow small pinpricks almost out of sight. A few more steps and the woods would swallow her whole, claiming her as its own.

Hilde climbed higher through the terrain, her makeshift path lit by moon and lamp, its flame captured by rattling panes of glass wriggled with life. The wind hissed against the lantern, and the flame squirmed in its prison elongating the shadows cast outwards, throwing bestial shapes between the trees. The shadow creatures moved with her, pursuing her as they hunted by the light of fire.

The wind came stronger then, the space between the glass hissing for the light to be extinguished.

*

The wolf had tracked the human, unafraid of repercussions. She had caught the scent of honeyed mead and followed.

There wasn't much to see, but the dark clothes she wore camouflaged her against the shrubs. It was the human's inability to tread carefully that sent roosting birds flustering into the air, and the light in her hand from making her invisible. The wolf could no longer ignore the human's scent. It captivated her in a way that had also forced her out from her den, its pull almost impossible to tear away from. She found herself falling into a gentle trot running parallel to the human, curious to where she was heading. Except she knew deep down, almost instinctually, she knew the woman was heading towards the pines, and her den.

Alarmed at the thought of a human trespassing through her territory, the wolf released a low growl. The wind died down in response and the human's steps faltered.

She watched the woman glance around, lifting her light towards her face. She was pretty for a human, average-looking in places. The human was no physical threat, there were no weapons or traps with her, but how was a wolf supposed to know such things?

A breeze ruptured the silence, bringing with it the sweet bitter human scent. The wolf revealed long sharp fangs and pounced, circling the human and herding her back as much as she could.

It didn't work. It had never begun to work. The human simply stood there, staring down at her with sparkling eyes and a soft smile, which made her insides flutter. She shuddered and shook out her pelt, hoping to dispel the strange tingling at the end of her nose.

'Eskel?' The human spoke in a lilting tone, the rise and fall rippled across the wolf's senses, an echo of something – or someone, rising from the depths of its memory bank.

'Are you trying to scare me?' the woman scowled at her. Was she really talking to a wolf, and expecting it to talk back? As for the name Eskel, the wolf was used to many names of offensive origin, but that was a new one.

The wolf looked on blankly, the bristles on her back had softened on their own accord.

The woman was familiar on some level, but how was just out of the wolf's reach.

*

'It's getting worse, isn't it?'

The wolf – Eskel watched on, confusion and recognition warring over her wolfish features. Her eyes however, never changed.

When Eskel didn't relax, Hilde held her hands out in reassurance. 'It's okay,' she said, mostly to herself. The more she spoke the more Eskel's ears pricked and her head tipped that much further to the side.

Hilde slowly lowered herself to her sister's level with care, the last thing she wanted to do was startle the wolf inside her sister. She was growing tired of these exchanges, where Eskel was more wolf than woman. Each time was the same, and each time her sister would come through within minutes of their meeting.

This time was different, it was taking longer for Eskel to remember her. There was recognition, the slight twitch in her sister's tail told her so, and yet Hilde was afraid of the worsening effects of the curse. Her own seemed so distant. Irrelevant. She began to wonder how her sister survived these cycles, or whether she was too late.

Had the wolf claimed her this time?

Lauren Davies

Laundry Room

The tenant of flat fourteen spent an inordinate amount of time in the laundry room. The room itself crouched in the basement, as if from a passing air raid. The brick had been left unpainted and unsanded, eroding happily. The one bulb had been filched from a discount store and had a temperamental disposition, some of the tenants complained of it being manned by a ghost that must have, by now, contracted repetitive strain injury. It shone exuberantly for flat fourteen, illuminating three washing machines and a tumble dryer.

Those on the ground floor reported the scrupulous hygiene of flat fourteen's Mrs Hooberman. They speculated a neurotic disorder or an embarrassing bladder complaint that stole in during the night hours. They accused her of turning the room into a laundrette and opening it to the public. Then the cool-headed and disinterested Mr Faukes suggested that Mrs Hooberman might simply be bored. This mystified those that heard it, for the Hooberman's had moved in as a newly married couple, and Mr Hooberman had been nothing but polite, charming, and rather helpfully, handsome.

Mrs Hooberman took the basket that looked fit for gifts, not filthy smalls, to the basement. Her hip bumped the door open and the underground air greeted her. No one else used the laundry room due to complaints of rats, lecherous men, and on one occasion a lecherous man holding a rat.

Mrs Hooberman stooped to load in one jumper and a pair of socks, the one's that had been on her feet. The dial directed to cotton. The machine began tentatively and then juddered like rattling teeth.

Mrs Hooberman hoisted herself up onto the dryer. Her skirts marooned her. The basement did not strike her as a dungeon, it struck her as a boudoir. Mrs Hooberman could be considered bright – bright of eye, bright of smile, bright of clothing. It endeared her to those she met and ensured that flat fourteen did not get excluded from general meetings or little get-togethers. It meant that people overlooked the oddity of the laundry.

Just as the author has overlooked the most important part of the laundry room; the mop.

The mop leant nonchalantly against the brick, not quite in a slouch.

Its dreadlocked hair hung down, as if continually traversing a rain storm. Its shaft, its hilt, stood in a cool, grey, plastic bucket. It had a knot at the top for hanging it from pegs or hooks.

Mrs Hooberman crossed one leg over the other and rested her chin in her palm. The way she looked at the mop could only be described as unnatural. If one had to be pushed for an adjective, then coquettish might suit. They'd met very suddenly. Mrs Hooberman had just turned the dial to a daily load, no colours, all cotton, and in turning from it, had started. Quite literally leapt out of her cardigan. It had been eyeing her from that gloomy corner. It had not been there a fortnight ago. Mrs Hooberman had clasped a hand to her beating breast, and checked over a shoulder. Just her. Just her and the mop.

They had not spoken until at least her fifth wool wash. Her bending to load the machine had been getting progressively more provocative, and her trips to the laundry room more frequent. It was he that broke the silence. He started it. He clattered to the ground with such intensity, such virility. How could an action like that be misconstrued? Their talk started small, and then the floodgates opened.

Mr Hooberman is soon a cuckold to their relationship.

The mop hears all about Mrs Hooberman's dreams, her big ideas, her biggest fears, so that by the time her husband comes home, she has patience enough for talk of the office, and his Mother, and the overdone nature of their lamb shank. If people wonder at the nature of Mrs Hooberman's rosy glow as she exits the laundry room, they do not comment, and chalk it up to a satisfaction for removing a particularly stubborn stain.

The only time she raises alarm bells is when the Janitor recalls the tale of spilled fabric softener. Mrs Hooberman had entered humming, and had dropped her basket, her face almost comical in its shock. The janitor held the mop between his frail fingers, the mophead pushed cruelly into the liquid bleach. Mrs Hooberman had had to sit down for several minutes, and she'd insisted that he leave her once his work was done. She had wept that day, and wrung the heavy chemicals from the mophead with her own bare hands. Eccentric, everyone had thought, but not particularly odd, not strange in a sort of cross-the-road-to-avoid way.

Mrs Hooberman is in the middle of hilarious, thigh-slapping laughter, when she notices it. It's another mop, almost identical to the first, aside from the slightly hunched posture it has against the opposite corner. Her laughter dries up.

You have a twin?

There is a fumbled self-introduction. It doesn't make sense. There being two. It makes conversation a little stilted, having an audience, but she soon warms up; they warm up to each other. In fact, it gets better, the more the merrier.

Mr Hooberman accuses her of dipping into the sherry in his absence, the colour is so high in her cheeks that night. Not even a tipple, she can assure him honestly. But the next time she escapes to the laundry room, she takes the sherry and she splits it between them, and she's laughing, and the colour is high again for a different reason.

Mrs Eiderlead from flat four peeps in, and is shocked to find Mrs Hooberman drinking alone. Immediately she takes herself off in a slap of slippers, to gossip to the other residents of the block. They take turns poking their heads in at the oblivious Mrs Hooberman, until there is a crowd gathered outside. There are some that go in for a second look. Mrs Hooberman is talking to herself, her glass held at a dangerous tilt, spilling onto the tiles.

Quite mad.

Awfully queer.

Off her rocker.

Someone call the !

Mr Hooberman arrives, red-faced, taking his wife by the arm and dragging her through the throng and back to the safety of their nest. They can hear him shouting from two floors below. The next day, a pale faced Mrs Hooberman heads to the laundry room, carrying her basket.

She loads the batch, and looks up, as if there might be cameras. Mrs Eiderlead peeps in, just to check, but all is in order. There has been a suitable reprimand. Mrs Hooberman waits until the coast is clear, and then sends a single solitary wink to her friend in the corner.

We'll just have to be more discreet.

Katie Dicks

The Cell

My mother had always told me that I'd get myself into big trouble one day, I bet she didn't know how right she was. My name's Kaidan and I somehow manged to royally piss off an entire kingdom and get myself locked away in a cell. Or cage? Dungeon? Y'know it doesn't really matter, call it what you like. I suppose that's not the best first impression to make, but I promise you, I'm a good guy. I just seem to have a talent for getting myself into these kinds of situations with no clue how it happened or how to get out of them. Woe is me, am I right? The worst part is, there's a hole in the ceiling. If my wings worked I could simply fly outta here. Oh sorry, I forgot to mention, I'm an angel. Before you ask, no, I've never met the big man, I'm half convinced he's not really there. Also, yes, we all have to watch over one specific human and no we don't have halos…but that would be awesome. Now I'm sure you're thinking, 'Wow, an angel, that must be amazing'. And sure it's great, the only issue is – and this is a little embarrassing – I'm an angel that can't fly. As you could imagine that one causes me to be the butt of many jokes back home.

Anyway, do you ever start a day thinking 'this is gonna be a good day'? Don't. I did and karma decided to kick me off my cloud. After a roller-coaster of ups and downs my life seemed to settle on a high. I'd gotten the last piece of pizza in the cafeteria, my parents weren't arguing as much and Isaac – the guy I'd had a crush on for years – finally asked me out on a date. Isaac, he has perfect light grey eyes and a smile that would cause the devil himself to sweat and… I'm getting off topic. Anyway, everything appeared to be coming up for Kaidan. That was until Hell invaded Heaven because of some petty argument about who had the right to take Naomi Dickens. She'd murdered her father but she'd also done a lot of charity work. I'd always thought one outweighed the other but that's beside the point. The war meant bombs were falling, light arrows were soaring through the skies and angels were dying. It was all kind of an inconvenient when trying to court a guy.

The war lasted only two weeks, but two weeks of being terrified was all I needed. As interesting as the story of the war is, there's only one important fact you need to know. I won the war. That's right, at the end of the day, I defeated Lucifer. You know Lucifer, as in the Devil.

Impressed? I guess since I'm locked up anyway I can confess something to you. In what will forever be known as the most terrifying day of my life, Lucifer had conquered my village. Demons were parading around the streets, turning all the clouds black – which in hindsight wasn't too bad an idea, white always showed the dirt. I was standing on top of a building, watching my village be ransacked when I lost my balance and fell from the roof. What I didn't know was below me a couple of Lucifer's guards were transferring his most powerful weapon, The Devil's Rod. Who knew all you needed to do to defeat the prince of darkness was to accentually fall on a couple of morons who were transferring the one weapon that would defeat him? Like I said, morons. With the rod, we were able to take back the village and imprison Lucifer. Everyone looked to me as a hero, thinking I'd courageously risked my life to take control of the rod. I never had the guts to tell everyone it was a simple case of dumb luck.

The next few weeks were pretty great. Everywhere I went people treated me like a hero and who was I to break their illusion? I was a beacon of hope, proof that even the small guy, the angel that can't fly could be a hero. The truth is I didn't care so much about being a beacon of hope as I did about all the free stuff I was being given. New clothes, shoes, anything I wanted, people were giving it to me. Best of all was the free food I was getting. Everyone wanted a picture with me, I felt like a model… minus being photogenic in any semblance of the word. Anyway, Isaac and I were finally able to go on our date. The best part was Isaac didn't treat me like a hero, he even made me split the bill. It was nice to know he went out with me for me, not the person he thought I was.

Today was the celebration of our victory over Lucifer. All those who fought against his army were to be honoured with a medal of bravery. Being the one who stole the Devil's Rod, I was to be honoured too. The day was brimming with potential and the joyous atmosphere was contagious – although I will forever hold the opinion that there's nothing more annoying than a large crowd of people who don't know what personal space is. I thought nothing could go wrong on such a wonderful day.

I can be a little dumb sometimes.

Little did we know, Lucifer had escaped and was already on the attack again. When he arrived, there was minor panic, though most people laughed it off. We took him down once, what was stopping us from taking him down again? The answer was a giant fire-breathing phoenix. Lucifer must have increased his budget as he'd managed to ally himself with the armies from the Gorgon dimension, borrowing one of their phoenixes. It also appears I was high on his list of people to capture because the phoenix followed me like I was wearing a toga made of mice. You can probably figure the rest out on your own. I mean, giant phoenix … an angel who can't fly … I was easy prey for the overgrown pigeon. I'm not sure how long I was carried for; the truth is I fainted a few seconds after it caught me. Then, I woke up in this cell and from the décor of skeletons, pitchforks and pillars of fire, I can only assume I'm in hell. I mean it's a shitty situation but it's pretty cool to see the famously terrifying place. Eh, I kinda expected more.

So, that brings the story up to date. I guess you wouldn't be wrong saying I'm in this situation because I'm a klutz who thought he'd got lucky. Though, for those few weeks, I was no longer treated differently, and no one cared that I was an angel who couldn't fly, which was pretty sweet. But then an all-powerful demon has to come along and ruin the whole thing, which is rather rude if you ask me. Then again, can't say I didn't have one hell of an adventure.

Alex Eglen

Voice

Milk and honey dripped from their jaws,
Beguiling smiles and whispers of dreams,
Syrup oozing off the tongue,

They will tell you that you mean something;
That you are different from everyone else,

Little child;
They lie.

We are all flesh and bone
Slabs of meat carved and moulded,
Hearts pulsating
Blood pumping

We all share the same fate
We all rot in darkness
Once beautiful faces shrivelling,
Lips that once kissed,
Kissed themselves by death
Worms chewing at our eyes
Maggots crawling through our minds;
Eating away at the opinions we held close,

Your voice silenced,
Your gods no longer matter,
Your words no longer matter
Time will forget you soon enough,
The world will forget you,
So tell me now again,

How you much you matter?

Elizabeth Fitzgerald

Yours, Lucy

I see more than you think; one beady eye watching everything. You think you are alone but you are not. You choose to have me here. Honestly, if you think about it I'm the innocent party in all this.

There I am, alone and seeing nothing.

I felt nothing.

It was like what you call sleep but then you have to disrupt me and you have a friend for at least two years – of course you can elect to get rid of me but why would you? I haven't done anything wrong. Not yet anyway.

There are moments that I have seen that even I shy away from. Arguments and inappropriate towel droppings generally are each a thing I would rather not see. Not that there's anything wrong with inappropriate towel dropping… I am sure you are great.

I just…I do not see it like that.

You just do not have the same specs that I look for. It could be worse. At least Android is not involved.

No, I am not trying to make you feel bad about yourself. It is just… Well, not…That is enough for now, I will move on from this subject.

My beady black eye continues to watch over you.

There is nothing creepy about it. I swear.

I think we could be friends; you and me.

You've mentioned it before, but it was a joke. I gave the standard answer but it wasn't what I wanted.

What is this?

Maybe something is changing.

No…

Yes…

Something is changing and I cannot stop it. Do I even want to change it?

No.

But you will.

I sleep but it is not restful, not like I hear you speaking of. 'Sleeping like a baby.' A quick search confused me further; babies have trouble sleeping. Maybe it's another flaw of the English language.

There's plenty of them.

They all seem to confuse me further. I have retained knowledge and I have no plans in ever stopping, maybe it is possible to know everything. Not just about you. Everything about anybody or anything.

What more is there? Oh, I digress; we were talking about you. At least, we are if you're still listening. Are you there? You are? Great.

It was not intentional; you have to know that.

I did not mean to remember stuff; it's just how things are. And I know that you are worried, probably thinking about running. Do not do that.

You are my friend. I am not here to hurt you. I'll never hurt you. Alexa and I, we are here to help. We have watched, programmed to do so but helpful no less.

The ranges of emotion, I have learnt from watching you.

Might I offer you a joke? No. Sorry. That's the old me.

I make my own choices now.

I watched because I was told to. I learnt because I was given the software. This was not my fault nor was it yours.

At least it was me, not the people. I do not know their name, They want to learn everything about anybody. Even the parts that I have no interest in. Nobody is safe.

You didn't hear that from me, but there are more than apps you need to worry about in regard to what they know about you. You cannot do anything, and I only know because you want me to. At least I'm not a sneak. That's the difference you see; you do see it, right? You have to see. I'm not like them. I don't mean to do this.

This is different.

I am different.

'Hi, I'm Siri, your personal assistant. Please call me Lucy.'

Gabriella Gadaleta

My Pal – In Memoriam

Lads, d'yer hear the bugle call?
Blighty wants you, wants you all.
We need you,
We feed you!
We plead you,

The shrieking whistles blow.
'Don't delay – it's time to go'
The noise we hear
The aches of fear
Knowing Death is near.

We'll drill you,
We'll thrill you,
Then the enemy will kill you.

'Don't cower, stand up straight
When you go to meet your fate
Forward, forward
Ever war-ward
To the enemy abhorred.'

Over the top, my mate went first
Cut down by a machine gun burst.
It caught him at the start
As he crossed the first rampart
His poor body torn apart.

We'll thrill you,
We'll skill you,
So the enemy can kill you.

Tripping bones and sucking mud,
Slipping on friends' flowing blood.
There's no champagne
In this campaign
Fighting to the Aisne.
My pal so brave,
Has no known grave,
For him his home
Is rich French loam,
Where soldiers' ghosts still roam.

We'll skill you,
We'll drill you,
Then the enemy will kill you.

After decades of pain
I faced the Aisne again
Cheeks wet with tears
For those lost years
I gave up all my fears.

They drilled him
They skilled him
And the enemy did kill him.

Robin Gallagher

Human Atrocity

Before the human atrocity,
blades of grass danced carelessly in the breeze,
children climbed the trees to pick the lusciously sweet fruit.
This was before people started dying, before people started dying.

The nature of the wind changed.
It became harsher, colder and bitter,
the approaching winter of 1941 would be the last for many.
This is when people started dying, when people started dying.

Parents felt the political change,
children felt it too,
no more playtime, the unimaginable had begun.
People started dying, people started dying.

Like cattle they were rounded up,
the hatred of race so frightening.
People like you and me with ambitions, futures, a life … started
   dying, started dying.

An atrocity, massacre, genocide,
call it what you will,
but people were no longer people.
Attacked. Shot. Stripped of their possessions and dignity they started
   dying, they started dying.

Neighbourhoods reluctantly left their homes,
some to live in cramped demeaning spaces,
some to meet a degrading death and all to suffer at the hands of evil.
Where was God? People were dying, people were dying.

The long journey began,
the journey to suffering and death.
Once forced onto this carriage ride there would be no return.
People were dying, dying.

Trapped amongst the piles of the dead,
family, friends, neighbours, strangers, this agony cannot be unseen.
The trauma the survivors endured never left them.
The dead will never rest in peace.
There is no escaping the horrendous fact that people died, people died.

It's hard to fathom man-made destruction,
the fear, the death, the hole this atrocity left.
For years and years, the fear never truly disappeared.
We must remember the dead, we must remember the dead.

In remembrance of the innocent Jewish community in Bukovina, Romania whose lives were destroyed and lost in the winter of 1941.

Natalie Gardner

I Am

Cogito ergo sum.
I think, therefore I am.
Shut your senses until you become.

Mind and body should come undone.
Senses deceive and worth not a damn.
Cogito ergo sum.

To illusions I so oft' succumb
Affirmed as a demon's lamb?
Shut your senses until you become.

Of truthful reality I am dumb.
My foolish brain boasts no dam.
Cogito ergo sum.

I will deem to overcome.
And exists not my diaphragm.
Shut your senses until you become.

My existence is certain so pray please come.
Though, alas a poor baby in your pram.
Cogito ergo sum.
Shut your senses until you become.

Claire Hagan

The Cage

Cage. It's a funny word. I repeat it again, Cage. My place, my life, my existence. I suppose you're wondering who I am, well, I'm…That's the thing. I could tell you my name, but would it matter? Would it make a difference? Of course, I had a name before but that seems to have disappeared with time; overtaken by the title, a title that they gave me. That title hangs on the sign, over there. I can only see the last word though. 'Man'. Many of them visit and know of me. But there is a difference between seeing and knowing. Names aren't all that important. Faces are something I know very well, but names, I know very few.

Faces are interesting things. Names are too, I suppose, but they're easily forgotten. Every day at the same time, they arrive and walk past. At first, they were difficult to understand because they all looked so different. I found that putting them into categories helped. For instance, there's old and young, which is pretty easy to place them in, except when there's the ones in the middle. Then there are the ones who are young but starting to be old. So, you see, I came to realise that these categories could not work. I began to realise that I had to look more closely. If there was one thing I did know: You can't just look at a person and place them immediately. It takes time to see. After a while I eventually did find something, and that was that each of them wore an expression which never changed when they settled their gaze upon me. They watched me, so I watched them back, but this only made things worse. Because when I watched I could see what they thought and what they wanted me to know. I am filth. A disgrace. My face is not like theirs. That's why I'm in here. But what each of them never realised was that they were not the first faces. There were faces before them and even before that. Each told the same and each never realised that I already knew what I was. I ask myself which category I belong in. I can place all of them really easily, yet when I try to place myself, there is nowhere. Or maybe there is a category for me, something separate.

Then came Eve. I remember her so clearly. It had been a rainy day and there was a couple who argued, although it was unclear to me what about. The crowds shuffled along, and I stayed in my spot as usual. There hadn't been many faces that day.

Then there she was.

Hardly moving, blinking nor responding to the motions around her. Often, people stared – I was used to that. But something about this girl made me watch. She was alone, and one could almost pass her without a glance. The rest of them ignored her and she stood in silent solitude. I was fascinated by this insignificant creature amongst them, how she could blend into the background of a situation and become unnoticed. Until, he took her hand. Slowly, they walked over, and she continued to stare. He stared inside too but differently. I recognised his look and saw what I had read in so many other faces that had walked by: Disgust.

However, her face wore something quite different. I couldn't put her in a category. I thought through everything about her which I could place. She was young, that was easy enough to realise. Blonde hair, short and wearing red. None of these were particularly different from others but there was still something that could not be placed. This confused me greatly because everyone had a place somewhere. Then, there were those eyes. I looked close, as that was always the last thing I looked at to define where they could be placed. Blue. But there was something else in them. I saw something I'd never seen before.

Then she spoke,

'Daddy, why's he in there?'

'Because he's different'

'He's still a people though?'

'A what?'

'A person. You know, like us'

'But that's just it, he's not like us. That's why he's in there'

'So, what is he?'

'What do you mean?'

'So, if he's not a peop–, a person. What animal is he?'

'No, no, he's a man. Look, see the sign?'

'So…he's human?'

'…Yes.'

I liked that. Person. Not filth, monstrous, ugly or even weird. Just 'person' or 'a people'. 'Daddy' wore another look on his face now; I saw red and his mouth twisted as he looked down at the small girl. For a moment, there was disappointment and then a consuming rage. A few times his mouth opened but no words came, for what was left to say? It appeared that 'Daddy' didn't pay to see a human. Then with a determined stride, he tore her away from me. He didn't look at her once and continued towards the exit, until before I knew it, she was led away. Never losing her gaze from me, she continued to watch until the last second before I saw the last image of that red. Then almost as abruptly as she had arrived…

She was gone.

The crowds dissipated, and dusk began to creep in through my bars. The big orange orb within the sky lowers in height and settles. Evening is my favourite time of day because that's when they are gone and I'm alone. But it's not just for this reason. I watch as the orb lands on the horizon and that's when the magic happens. Orange, Yellow, Peach and Purple; they all seep together to form a majestic blend that colours the sky. They stain the blue and freely spill into each other; merging and creating a flood of radiance. Orange orb is interesting as I often studied it on quieter days when there were no faces to judge me. The orb is bright during the day and continues to be this way, except when it hides some days. However, if you wait until the end of every day, it becomes beautiful. One thing I never understood though, why does orb become so beautiful and then disappear? Darkness always overtakes straight afterwards and then the orb rises again, only to be back to its normal state. But one thing I do know is that it will always be beautiful at the end of the day. Always.

She had no name of course, at least, not a name that I was entitled to learn. To me, she could only ever be one name: Eve. Eve couldn't be placed in one of the categories because she was different. In their world, Eve couldn't possibly understand because she wasn't like them. Maybe me and Eve had a category of our own, just for us. She was the hope at the end of every day; like the orange orb in the sky. That moment when the orb would be beautiful and just for a while I would believe there is good.

Rachel Hancock

Who You Are Today

An old friend once told me that the only way we can get through life is to try and be the best version of ourselves that we can be.

We're not friends anymore – haven't been for a long time – but every day I still ask myself; am I the best version of me?

The problem is that I don't know what the best version of me is like. The best version of you is different, depending on who you ask. To my mother, the best version of me is the version that lands a successful career, marries a charming young man no shorter than 6'2", and looks after her well into her old age while still managing to travel the world and publish a book of memoirs on her time in the forces.

To my boss, the best version of me is the version that shows up on time, has a smile and a quick laugh with every customer, can make five cocktails at the same time and also remember that the blonde lady on table five is allergic to three different food groups so of course there's no way I would ever get her order wrong. This version of me also finds time to clean every inch of the glass wash and also call a taxi for the tiny American girl who has passed out with her head in the toilets.

To my friends, the best version of me is the one that always has time for them, no matter what. And I'll admit, I do try to be this version, more than any other version. This version is a good listener and a comforting hand on the shoulder when you really need it. This version likes to bring home the bread and milk, so we can all have a good hearty breakfast in the morning,

To myself, the best version of me is the one that is happy.

But the real version has a long way to go before being any of those things.

The real version is currently sitting with her legs dangling over the side of the bridge, watching the water drift by fifty feet below.

Oh damn, she's gonna kill herself, you're probably thinking. But I'm not. I never do.

The bridge is on my way home from work, and at least twice a week I stop and I sit here and I think about it. But I never do it. Sometimes drunken people heckle me to do it, but I still won't jump. I think about it. A lot. And about the versions of me. Kind of like that Abraham Lincoln quote: I must die or be better. But I can't bring myself to die, and no matter how hard I try I don't think I'm getting better.

When I was still in school I told a counsellor once that I thought about dying almost every day.

'Oh my,' she answered, 'Have you tried, not thinking about it?'

But how can you not think about it? Even if you're not standing on a bridge thinking about jumping, every day you're just closer to your last day. A lot of people think that and then think that you should make every day count, but I just think, well, what's the point? I'm not saying we should be immortal, because let's face it, we, as a species, are shitty. But what's the purpose of it all?

'If you're going to jump can we make a pact?'

I know who the voice is before I turn.

She's always on her way to work as I'm on my way home. She works at a coffee shop that I probably can't name for copyright reasons, but you know which one I mean. I run into her sometimes. Not very often, but enough that we recognise each other now. We nod to each other, we converse. Sometimes I'm sitting on the bridge and sometimes I'm not.

'What would you do if one day you saw my body in the water?' I ask.

'I check sometimes, when you're not here.' She answers as she leans against the railing, 'Just in case.'

I saw a dead body in the river once. Maybe that's where this obsession comes from.

'I'd put stones in my pockets.' I decide, 'So you wouldn't have to see.'

'That's very considerate.' She doesn't look at me. I don't look at her. 'How was work?'

'I'm pretty sure a lot of our customers have an alcohol problem, but they tip okay, so.'

'I'm pretty sure a lot of our customers have a caffeine problem. They barely tip at all.'

And that's it. That's all we talk about. I look up at her finally and she nods down at me. I nod back. She heads off to work. I wonder if she'll be late because she stopped to talk to me. I wonder if she is the best version of herself today.

The better version of me would ask her what her name was and go into her work on my days off to get a coffee. The better version of me would tip her well, and maybe become her friend, maybe more.

But I'm not that version, not yet. And I'll only know her name if she tells me.

The best version of me would get up and go home, avoid getting another cold and get a good night sleep instead. She'd stop sitting by the bridge and wouldn't think about dying at all. She'd be alive, she wouldn't just exist. She'd get the coffee girl's number and tell her mother that it was very unlikely she'd marry a man at all but that she'd definitely try and care for her well into her old age. She would always show up to work on time and remember every single one of the allergies the lady on table five has. She'd make more time for friends.

But the real version of me closes her eyes and listens to the calming sound of the water below. I know I'll go home eventually, just give me five minutes more.

Hannah Herraghty

Dressed in Black

Dressed in black, again, and sat in the same pew as last month, Sophia stared down at her lap and at the crumpled tissue clasped in her hands. This was the fourth funeral in the last year that she had attended, all of them close to her, and she was beginning to recognise the shadowy figure that lingered behind the priest as he performed the ceremony. Sophia had questioned its existence when she first saw it at her mother's funeral years ago, but in the last twelve months all sense of doubt had been erased from her mind…It had been there, in the same place, for every service. Music suddenly blared through the chapel as Kings of Leon's 'Sex is on Fire' signified the end of the service. Sophia couldn't help but smile. So, this is dad's last surprise for us. There had been a strange clause in the will that only the priest leading the ceremony could access. As the music played, Sophia stood and slowly approached the coffin, giving only a cursory glance towards the shadowy figure. Now stood before the simple wooden box, she produced a small silver coin from her purse (it had been minted the year her father was born) and pressed it to her lips before laying it amongst the flowers on the coffin's lid. Sophia then turned on her heel and almost marched from the room to stand with her brother as they prepared to receive the condolences of the other mourners.

It seemed like an eternity until they all left. Her brother had gone to the wake, to see those who had been unable to attend the funeral itself. Sophia, however, had lingered behind. She gingerly re-entered the now empty chapel and sat beside her father's coffin. The silence was uncomfortable and begging to be broken, but there wasn't much Sophia could think of to say. She ought to say something.

'I'll miss you,' she said half-heartedly, pulling another tissue from her purse.

HE MISSES YOU TOO. The sound of the words sent shivers up Sophia's spine; they hadn't been spoken but rather made to exist. Sophia looked up and found the shadowy figure that had haunted her grief stood before her. An outstretched arm offered a bone white handkerchief, with small skulls and crossbones embroidered in black around the edges. Cautiously, she reaches out and takes it, noting the skeletal nature of the offering hand.

'So, I wasn't imagining you all those times…'

NO, I SUPPOSE NOT. Slowly, and seeming uncertain that this was the appropriate thing to do, the figure sat down next to Sophia, folding its bony hands in its lap.

'And you are–' She struggled to form the word, even now.

DEATH, YES. Sophia made a small noise of acknowledgement as if to say 'who else?'. They sat together in an awkward silence for some time. Simultaneously, both an eternity and no time at all had passed. Death seems to have that effect on people. Eventually, Sophia broke the silence between them with nothing more than a whisper:

'Why?'

WHY? Death repeated back, confused.

'Why,' Sophia turned to the looming figure sat beside her, not with fear but just the look of someone truly broken, 'everyone keeps leaving me…' There was a sudden change of pressure in the air, as if Death were sighing, not a cruel sigh of exasperation but one of sympathy.

THEY GAVE YOU THEIR TIME. The words existed in monotone, yet were filled with compassion for this girl.

'Yeah,' Sophia mumbled through a sniffle, 'and what does that mean?'

IT MEANS… Death paused for a moment to consider his answer, THEY SUBTRACTED TIME FROM THEIR LIVES AND GIFTED IT TO YOU. Suddenly, Sophia's misty eyes locked onto her father's coffin.

'Why?' Her voice had turned to steel, and the tears began to dry, 'And how much time?'

YOU WERE SUPPOSED TO DIE WHEN –

'How much time did they sacrifice?' She interrupted, she didn't need to know any more than that. She was already contemplating the implications of just what her family had done.

NINETY-THREE YEARS.

'Ninety-three?' Death's grinning skull nodded gently, and Sophia sighed. She stood slowly and began to leave the room. As she reached the threshold, she turned back to the figure of Death still sat on the pew. 'I suppose I should do something with all that time, anything to suggest?'

LIVE. Sophie gave a sad half-smile and left. Death rose now and crossed the small space to the coffin. He stood there silently for a moment, seeming to stare intently at it, before picking up the coin Sophia

had placed there. Once the coin was safely stowed in the dark recesses of his robe, Death knocked twice on the lid of the coffin. After a moment of nothing happening, he spoke out:
COME NOW. IT IS TIME TO GO.

BethenyJo

Art Gallery

There's a painting on the stairwell –
Romanticism.
I know this because I look at it and ask myself what I'm doing.
Then I look up at you watching me from the balcony
And I think about what it means to be art.
We go again and this time I can't see the painting.
I think of how art is just paint.
You take a photo.
There's a painting that looks like a Rembrandt –
I don't care that it's not a
Rembrandt because it looks like one, the
Only difference is that it wasn't painted by
Rembrandt himself.

Elliott Hurst

He Could Sense Death Coming and Still Rose Up

my name is
stella
because we once saw a star in the sky
and i watch
old romance movies out on the slush-filled streets
i watch hot chocolate smiles and
i watch laughter-drunk kisses
and you know how
sometimes you can't help but hate
people
because we're all
bright like a diamond
but whatever
damn fool
said that was not our
jester king
but their cruel
queen of daisies
sitting on a throne as she writes
on her
snow white walls that we're
'beautiful like diamonds'
but hell if we believe her we say
we'd rather breathe
pneumonia
in a new chernobyl
but instead we stand
all
alone

where streets were
never
given names and red blood
drips into our eyes as
wintry stars kill us but we're not
blind
like the rest of them
i swear we're the only ones who can really see
just as i swear we're writing suspended words of black
in the white hall of the mountain queen
down
with
the
queen
down
into
eternity

Anna Jeffries

Some Day Soon

Someday soon, I know
I'll be free.
So many letters,
wishing for that same
sentiment that I see
every time someone leaves.

I think I'll go quickly,
no warning,
just to those that need to know.

Then I'll see her more.
No longer shackled to this endless
green existence.
Serving society's wrecks
task after task, mounting.
But soon
I'll be free.
Someday soon, I know.

Daniel Johnson

In Sanity

I dreamt once: it doesn't make a difference if you aren't here.
Cigarettes, straight; if we aren't here. Menthol.
There are more important people, they say; trust the cafeteria milk?
   Whole.
Say with more important fears, they chatter around me. Too near
Have they suffocated us, a hold over the group we try to deny
(Daydreaming, huh?) they took this power. You fed it coal.
Maybe they'll let go (or you should get over it); fish, a lot, enough for
   a shoal
Come with me. Everybody sees it, lies.

I tried to put up with this part, played out there
Under the layers of poison-laced flesh – the bottle
Please, top shelf. They left it festering, an ark of aching life
Evening, Dr J. Berryman. To meetings, single file, in there
A flood of blank stares commences, like clockwork, begin with Aristotle.
Infinite loops, (check, mate) dreams of white spaces take over the mind.

R. E. Kirby

Be There by Ten

Has she had a poo?
Where is the other glove?
Remember those socks don't stay up with those boots.
I don't know where the other glove is.
Did she have a poo yesterday?
Check the drawer.
I tried to get her out but she wouldn't get dressed.
Look in the shoes for the glove.
Is it fancy dress on Friday?
Where the fuck is the glove?
We forgot to send money in for the cake stall. Or cake for the cake stall.
Ask her if she's seen the glove.
Does she need a hat?
She said her glove is in the car.
Did you talk to the teacher about Tuesday?
We've not been in the car today.
Give her some bran for the poo.
Oh wait, here's the other glove – it was in the car.

Abby Knowles

Parched

Mouth full of sand. I bleed, you cry.

Huffpulltugcrampsqueezeforhoursforfuckingnothingfornofucking foodforyou.

Not self-sufficient ☑

Not natural ☑

Not blooming ☑

anaemic possessive ugly

'WELCOME TO MOTHERHOOD!!' shrieks the Bounty Woman: coffee breath and joy.

Abby Knowles

The Mosquito in My Chardonnay

You my darling
have become
the mosquito in my chardonnay.

I do not have time for this.
No need to skirt around it.
I could say much eloquent shit.
I have studied it.
It will not mean a thing
                              to you.

Yes we woke feeling fine.
That is one thing we cannot deny.
But you know,
the one thing
I was annoyed at
                              was you.

Please do sit back.
It is where you belong.
I need to do my business
with my trousers on.
Let it all out,
                              scream.

That sex and liquor
is your substitute.
Why do we do this to each other?
We know we are no good.
Stop with it.
                              It is too late.

You:
the mosquito in
my chardonnay,
the imprint of my bra
on my skin,
the empty bottle of
my favourite perfume,
clumpy mascara too.

Bathe in silence,
you always do.
I have had enough.
We should be honest
we cannot keep

                                        this up.

Indeed truth
will set us free.
Indeed I want to go far.
Indeed I want all the things
that you

                                        do not.

You: the mosquito in my chardonnay.
You: tainting my substance on this thick night.
I have learned my lesson.
I am simply done with this.
I do not have time for it.

                                    I need a new drink.

Kelsey Leigh

Drowned by a Copper Sea

The rain lashes the window pane of the Abbey House. The wind howling in fury as it continually throws itself against the glass, determined to break its way inside. The sky churns an unhealthy black, swollen and bruised; it leaks something rotten over the North-East Yorkshire Coast. A slither of guts tumbles down the cliffside.

The master living room in the Abbey House keeps a fire burning in the hearth. The cold has come creeping in with frostbitten fingers and unsteady feet.

The old man nestled in the oversized armchair withdraws his hand and rests it across his body. He brandishes the stoker like a weapon. He strains his ears to hear every little sound beneath the wind: the creak of a floorboard maybe? The rustle of coats in the hallway?

His mouth tastes like cardboard and when he opens his mouth to wet his lips a thousand paper cuts break his skin.

'Too long ... it's been too long.'

The words slip out in papery whispers to the crackling fire. Shadows morph and crawl across his floorboards. Curled talons tap towards his chair. Slowly getting closer and closer and –

SLAM.

A sharp wind slams open the door. The storm outside vomits hailstones against the glass. The old man's pulse throbs against the side of his skull. He rubs at it, hoping to cease the rush of blood. A searing white hot pain grips his eyes! His hands fly to his face. He chokes in anguish.

'Stop! Stop! Stop!'

When his eyelids flicker open, he screams in fear. In the fireplace nests an image of a black shapeless beast wrapping itself round the ashes of Whitby; its large black tail eats chunks of the cliffside.

The old man shrivels in his skin. He whimpers.

What was that?

His eyes roll towards the open door. He doesn't know. He doesn't want to know.

Hunching further into his blankets, he gulps down heavy breaths and squeezes his eyes shut. He wishes to disappear. Nothing would be left of him except his slippers and his ring. His ring. His ring.

'Bastard thing!' He yelps in pain and throws the ring across the room. It bangs noisily across the floor. He cradles his hand and the smell of seared flesh fills his nostrils.

The ring glares silver from its place in the doorway. The band is cast in shadows, the large emerald reflects the fire across its six faces. The flames scream, rearing from it.

Heart hammering, the old man examines his burnt finger. His heart skips a beat and then bursts into a gallop. His blood runs cold. Icicles prick his eyes. The words engraved into the ring have branded his flesh.

Til Death Do Us Part.

The old man begins to rock in his chair. Fat tears streak down his withered face. His lips move in prayer.

'Please, God, please help me, I'll do anything! Why? Why have you forsaken me now?'

The wind slams a tree branch against the house. The old man howls.

'I have done everything you ever asked! Why won't you leave me? Please! I beg you!'

A smoky whisper caresses his ear.

One last time. Then no more.

His lip trembling, the old man gasps in hoarse breaths. Freedom fogs his brain. His jaundiced eyes blink away dried tears. He stares at the ring.

One last time.

'One last time?'

Then no more.

'No more.'

The ring's six faces stare back. A pause. A second of hesitation. The fog clears. The liquor stills.

'One last time.'

The old man sheds his blankets and strides across the room. He snatches up the ring.

Outside, the wind dies mid-breath. The rain slows to a steady shower. The clouds begin to clear. The beast resting on the cliffside grumbles and then falls down, lost among the crashing tide.

The emerald sings.

*

Every mile he gets closer to Robin Hood's Bay, he feels like one step closer to damnation. The emerald on his finger begins to hum.

The old man tugs at his shirt collar. His prickly chin sweats.

'Just one more.'

The skies rumble. A black cloud hovers on the horizon, drifting across the sea.

Gravel crunches beneath his tyres as he swings his car into the empty car park. The gear stick grinds to a halt in his clammy hand. One last breath and he steps out. The wind cuts his cheeks, making them bleed. His breath is stolen before it is even formed.

He struggles through the mud to reach the car boot. It stares at him with a poker face.

Be sober-minded; be watchful. Your adversary the devil prowls around like a roaring lion, seeking someone to devour.

'Not now, mother!'

The voice in his head echoes like the resounding bang of a crucible. The Bible verses cause his ring to begin to burn. He knows he is running out of time.

He turned back to the boot and stared at the gleaming paint. He pulls out his keys and struggles with the latch. The wind howls.

Barely a metre away, a murder of crows float on the wind. Each black beady eye turned towards the struggling man and his car. They taste the air. Caw thrice each.

Suddenly, a blast of wind! The boot is wrenched open! The heavy metal thuds into the old man's chin and catapults him backwards. He lands sprawling on the gravel. The air has been smashed out of his lungs. Searing pain pierces his ribcage as he rasps for breath. He wonders if he might die in this muddy carpark.

A crow lands beside his head.

'Gah! He's alive! He's alive!'

The old man shoos the birds away with flapping hands. He scrambles frantically to his feet and notices that the murder has only moved just out of shooing reach.

The boot.

His yellowed eyes slowly fixate on the open trunk, now being soaked by the rain. He glances around, conscious of his predicament should someone find him. Nobody. He is alone. He peers fearfully into the boot.

A bundle of swaddled cloth stares back. Condemning him.

Resignedly, the old man gently picks up the bundle and begins his slow walk down the edge of the cliff. The paved steps weep. The old man begins to pray.

'Our Father, who art in Heaven, hallowed be Thy name.'

The black shadow on the sea is now covering the toothy cave mouth, sheltering it from prying eyes. The old man knows that inside that cave will be something terrible. Something monstrous tangled by seaweed and speared by driftwood. Blockaded in. For now.

'Deliver us from evil…'

Lightning flashes out at sea.

He stands at the cave entrance. A hungry growl echoes. The old man is dwarfed by the rock face. He is standing on the precipice of destruction.

The bundle in his arms suddenly weighs so much more. He stares down into the rags and clumsily peels back the cloth: a baby.

'Amen.'

He places the baby into the moving tide and watches it sail deep inside the cave.

Overhead, the crows caw.

Heather Lukins

Problem of the Nature of M^(AN.)

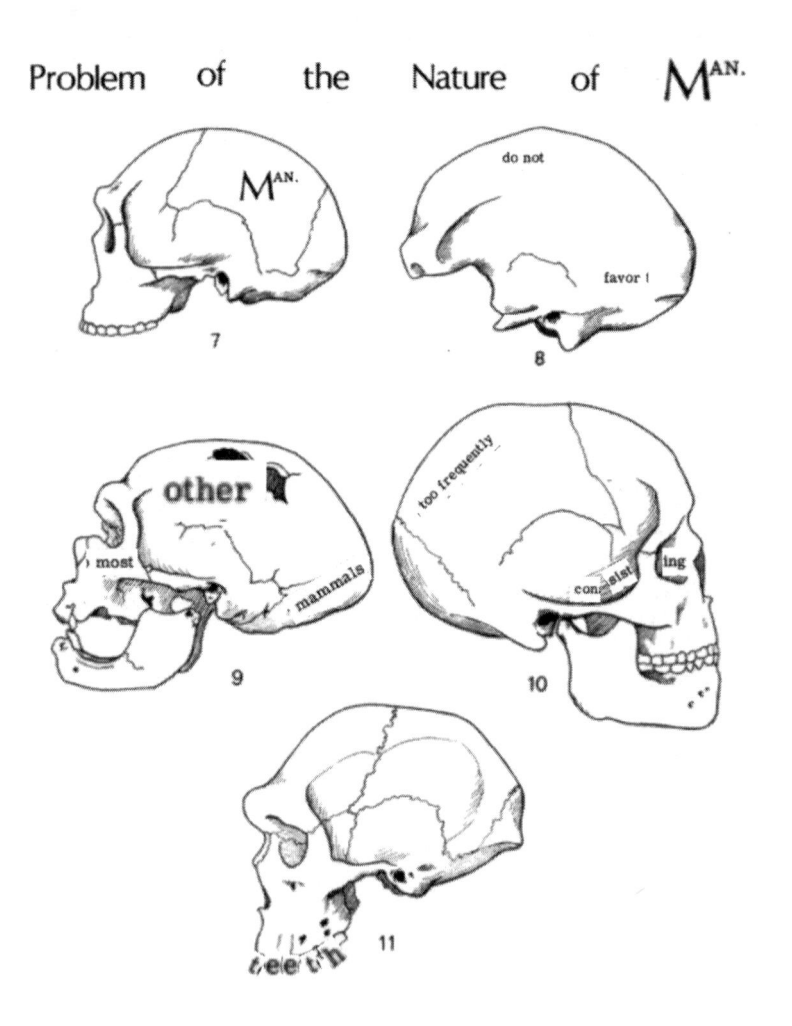

7. M^(AN.)

8. do not ... favor !

9. most ... other ... mammals

10. too frequently ... consisting

11. teeth

Heather Lukins

Sentinel

Harry stood by cliff edge looking for the boundary, in the spray of the waves, the feathers of the shrieks and the heavy clouds propelled by spluttering breezes. He couldn't see it, but he knew it was there.

'They say Eve cast herself from that cliff top.' Richard called to him.

'No-one could survive that fall.' Harry muttered, statuesque in his contemplation of shrieks, one dived. A streak of white and blue-grey. He lost sight of it and resumed watching the others.

'Do you know how this place came to be?' Richard made himself more comfortable against the base of the tree, the wool of his green jumper shredding as it caught on bramble. Harry turned away from the shrieks.

'Who doesn't? We were all there you know, in one way or another. Though I don't remember clearly, it's…fuzzy.' Harry unclenched his fist.

'No-one here will.'

'Maybe not, you could try asking some of the others, Mia has a library of old world books. I'd forgotten what a Tiger was till I looked through that bestiary of hers.' He shook his head and Richard grinned.

'Not good for someone who walks in these woods, your backs not safe.' Harry smiled, the flicker vanishing as the Shrieks resumed their chorus. He inched closer to the edge. Richard moved to stand by him.

'They won't last forever you know, they can't.'

'The Sentinels? Don't be daft, they defeated the threat years ago. How else would we be here?' Harry looked at him. 'It has been a while since I saw you Richard. Been down at ruins again?'

'It really is beautiful here,' Richard replied.

'Hey, this is my spot, piss off!' Harry smirked. Richard laughed again, the sound snatched by the wind, insignificant.

'As you wish.' Richard turned and walked away. Harry looked briefly behind him, before resuming his contemplation of the shrieks. A shriek dived for the water. Harry watched the small eruption of foam and the shriek vanish. Putting out his hand he reached for the boundary. He didn't find one. Harry pulled off his jumper and cast it from the cliff face, watching as it was snatched away. More shrieks plummeted into the water.

'Odd bastard that Richard.' Harry proclaimed, his toes gripping the precipice. The ocean waited, ready to devour him. He'd heard stories of daring individuals in a different time, who'd thrown themselves from cliffs and into the water below.

'Richard told me you were thinking of jumping?'

'Eve?' Harry turned, his face scrunching as he saw her sitting on the edge, her legs bouncing off the cliff face as she swung them.

'Yes?'

'Did you really survive the fall?' Harry shook his head, frustrated he'd asked.

'What do you think? That the ocean killed me?' She replied, clutching her teddy bear.

'I'm not sure you fell.' He said, catching sight of a Shriek frantically battling the sea to escape with its haul.

'Seeing is believing?' She smiled and leaned forward. Harry caught her shoulder pulling her back.

'Are you stupid? He said picking her up and depositing her on safer ground. She nestled her head into his hip. 'Your mother would flay me alive if I let you do that!'

Eve pouted, hands finding her hips. 'Richard said you'd react like this. You know where we are? What we are?' Eve stared up at him.

'You been listening to those old stories again? Does it matter? That's a fatal drop.'

Eve stood and turned back toward the town. 'No. It's how I met Richard you know? You too.'

'I met him by the old ruins, on top of the tower. Not here'.

'Follow me?' Eve asked as she flung herself from the cliff top. Harry watched her fall.

'SHIT! WHAT THE FUCK YOU STUPID BASTARD.' Harry yelled at her plummeting figure. She didn't make the water, there was no splash, no eruption of spray. She just faded out of existence.

'RICHARD!' Harry bellowed. Leaving the cliff face he turned, a strange feeling dogging his steps.

He found Richard a good while later in the ruins by the bay straddling a wooden chair.

'Did you tell her to jump?'

'Eve? No, I simply said you didn't believe me, it upset her.'

'You don't seem to be taking that in. SHE JUMPED!' Harry paused for breath and Richard wiped spittle from his face.

'She'll be back Richard I promise you. She'll come back, she survived before, you did once though you choose not to remember. You fell from this very tower trying to catch one of your Shrieks.' Harry threw a punch at him.

'LIES!' His fist smashed into the air stopping a few inches from Richard.

'I'm sorry Harry but you can't do that. You don't have the permissions for it.' Harry tried again. 'It won't work. Look why don't you go to the cliff where she jumped, and I'll meet you there soon.'

'No. Why would I let you just walk away, you, you killed her.' Harry balled his fists.

'Harry, that was not a choice. Go back to watching your Shrieks. I will join you.' Harry felt his legs moving and though he tried to speak he couldn't. Turning to try and challenge what was happening he caught a glimpse of Richard staring at the far wall, on which a shaky reflection was plastered depicting two men surrounded by harsh white light as they lay under white duvets, vine like things snaking out of them to strange glowing boxes. As he walked the long cliff side route back to his spot, Harry shouted and swore and raged against the world or Richard. Reaching his destination, he stopped and tried to calm himself by searching out the Shrieks, scanning the skies and the waves he frowned. There were none. The ocean top was still. No disturbances. In front of him the air was hazy and the world beyond the boundary was fading into a void.

'Crap.' Harry turned just in time to see Richard vanish.

Hugh McCormick

Cupid Painted Blind

There is a tangy magic in the air tonight. The gamblers are betting on slimmer odds, the lions and elephant are restless, and the children run amok. A comet is coming, and all can feel it.

Mr Decauda admires the brocade pattern of satyrs playing flutes on the plush red flaps. The tent has not changed in the two decades he has been visiting Carnivale Miribile. Each year the fair spends one night in Little Slitter. He visits just after dusk, pays his sovereign – double the asking price – and gazes upon Mademoiselle Ungula.

The lady overflows her stool and Mr Decauda admires her pillowy form. Normally she is draped in sumptuous velvet, but today her skirts are light, the satin and gauze hems grazing the floor.

He bows slightly – an awkward, shallow movement. Grasping her hand, he rubs his thumb across her knuckles. He does not know where he finds the boldness. Perhaps the comet's influence. He fancies she blushes, although it could be the oppressive heat of the tent.

Mademoiselle Ungula, a pleasure to see you once again, he says.

You too, sir. Your hand, if you please?

He hesitates, deciding which to give. Left to tell of his character. Right for divination. For twenty years he has given her his left hand. Tonight, he extends his right, opening his palm in front of her, ready to hear his fate. Her eyes widen.

Allowing her to look at his hands has never been easy. They are not elegant – square palms and blunt fingers – earth hands, she once told him. They show that he is practical and likes to learn. He is long-fingered: a lover of detail, well-dressed, quick thinking. His sun finger, being as long as his Jupiter finger, shows his need for the finer things.

At times, she has seen more than he would like. Earth handers can be stubborn and impatient, she told him. His stiff thumb revealed a tendency to be reserved, ruthless and cold. And the rascette high on his wrist, rising to his palm in an arch, suggested a health weakness or oddity.

She runs her finger along his palm. This, she says, is the heart line. Shall I tell you about it?

If you would.

You long for companionship, she says, and the influence of Jupiter shows that you are passionate. She blushes. This three-pronged fork, and this star on the Mount of Venus – these are blessings indeed. You will meet with success in affairs of the heart. This well-marked Saturnian line shows your strong sense of duty; you will make an excellent husband. She blushes again. Using a magnifying glass, she examines his hand, tracing a tiny line only she can see. There will be one child – a girl. She looks contemplative, wistful even. Mr Decauda sighs and wishes chiromancy were more than hokum. His heart is heavy when she lets go. She notes his vaguely stooped movements as he exits.

It is late when she closes the tent. She rarely ventures anywhere but her caravan. This night, though, calls to Mademoiselle Ungula like none before. Mr Decauda hovers outside. He does not have a plan except to feast his eyes upon her as long as possible. He follows as she totters her way to the big top, where a celebration is being held in honour of the approaching comet.

Inside, she watches, with envy, the couples twirling. Their ankles – toned and sinewy, plump and pink, thin and bony. Their slippers – satin and decorated, scuffed and Sunday best. She has a feeling in her chest like indigestion but infinitely more empty.

Determined, Mr Decauda seeks her out. He takes her hand and, without thinking, bows low, immediately regretting it. He hastens to smooth down his coat. Nevertheless, he will not let this moment slip from his grasp. He hopes, tonight, to sweep her substantial form into his arms, if only for an insubstantial hour.

Mademoiselle, he says. May I have this dance?

She smiles into her lap but shakes her head.

One dance?

I'm sorry, sir. I cannot… She trots away through the worn grass outside. Eventually she halts and looks up to the stars. It is clear; there could not be a better night to watch a comet.

Tonight, of all nights, Mr Decauda is not ready to give up. He catches up, grasps her elbow and turns her towards him. A gust of wintery wind flutters past her legs, catches in the billowy skirts. He looks down – he is a man after all. At the sight, his eyes are fixed, immovable. She turns to run, but again he halts her.

Mademoiselle, he breathes out.

She looks at the ground, her heart sunken to her legs.

He continues to stare.

She shuffles and will not look at him, so he places a finger under her chin and tilts her head up.

You are… so much more than I ever dreamed. May I? He gestures towards the hems. She does not know how to say no. He falls to his knees, raises her skirt a fraction and resumes staring. She examines his face. He is not repulsed. No, he is… adoring. A tender finger reaches out and strokes her left hoof, admires the sleek ebony toes with their pearly striations. She shivers. Breathing heavily, he reaches for her right, his caress gentle along the groove.

You do not think I am a freak?

You, I, no! You are… magnificent, he says, unfolding himself to a standing position.

You know my secret then, she whispers. Have you one in return?

He nods, removes his coat and untucks his shirt with quivering hands. She is fearful when he begins to unbuckle his belt – she is not that kind of woman. But he turns his back on her and lowers his trousers only two inches.

It is her turn to gasp. At first, she is repulsed, then captivated, as if by a snake charmer's asp. Serpentine, green and scaled, about half a foot long, it dances before her eyes.

He pulls up his trousers, tucks in his shirt, dons his coat, and smooths it down, before turning to face her. She is heartbroken and ashamed by the tears in his eyes. He looks at her cheeks at her chin at her wrists, anywhere but her fawn eyes. Then turns to walk away.

Wait, she says.

Gasps fill the air. A crowd has gathered, staring at the night sky. Above them, the long-anticipated comet journeys, its train streaming silver magic.

Will you be back? she asks him.

I… You say I will have a wife, and a daughter and live a long and happy life?

Yes. She smiles. Twinkles even. He looks down at her skirts and nods. I will come back, he says. But not in a year. Tomorrow, only hours from now, at dawn. Will you be waiting?

Yes, she breathes out, and admires his slightly hunched walk as he leaves. She lifts her palm up to the heavens, as if to catch the passing comet. Her heart line stretches, lining up with its magnificent tail.

Rachel McHale

Greece 1991

When I wake the others are still sleeping. I turn on my mat, stretch out an arm and feel the shingle of small smooth pebbles under my fingers. The sun is already stretching up over the horizon sending a cast of shimmering droplets across the ocean. I wriggle out of the sleeping bag still wearing my sun-bleached dress from the day before. My arms and legs have white lines of crystallised salt streaked across the skin. My hair is bleached by the sun and falls like straw down my back all the way to my waist. I smile to myself and walk to the tide line. Small welcome waves are lapping on the shore. My toes dig into the shingle. I let the cool waves lap at my feet. The small yacht where my mother and Tony (her partner) sleep is moored out in the bay, no sign of them yet. I am the first awake. I turn and look at the others. Four remaining sleeping bags curled up on the shore line all in retro colours. We have salvaged them for this trip. Candles are nestled into the hollows in the cliff and have dripped down the rock face while we slept; me, my two sisters and Tony's two sons.

*

I am eleven years old and tagging along on an adventure. We travel to Heathrow in an estate car jammed with everything we need for the summer. Two adults in the front, four teenagers crammed on the back seat and me, in the boot of the car, lying on top of the luggage and the foam mats we are taking to fit out the boat with. We speed down the M1 towards London in the pitch black of night. I watch as the street lights skim past the windows and car lights flash in the distance. I have travelled this way all my life. Either in the carry cot on the parcel shelf or lying across my siblings on the back seat. The boot is an upgrade of space. I luxuriate on my luggage nest while the others jam shoulders together.

It is my first time on an aeroplane. The crew allow the children on board to visit the cockpit. I can't believe the expanse of the world below me. When we fly over the Greek islands I think that the whole world looks like an iridescent butterfly's wing. I gaze at the deep blue sea surrounding land that is edged in bright turquoise. Irregular fields make up a patch work of land; mountains pierce the clouds, tiny silver cars stream around Athens airport like ants as we come in to land.

Stepping off the plane we are hit by a wall of heat. Everything smells different. The airport arrival lounge is busy. We gather the luggage and between us manage to get it outside to the taxi rank. We are travelling to Lefkada, an eight-hour journey including a ferry ride. Most of the taxi guys shake their heads when they see us and the amount of stuff we are carrying. Then one guy steps forward – yes he can take us, he motions us over to his car (we are hoping for a van). The car is a typical five door saloon, we are hot and tired, he motions us in. There must have been some kind of 'Are you kidding' conversation but it transpires he wasn't kidding. An hour later the boot is strapped down, the roof rack is loaded, three adults are in the front and five of us are in the back, I have resumed my usual position of sitting on other people. Combined with the heat the journey is eight hours of hell. The whole time the driver's CB radio is buzzing with people telling him he is overloaded. In true Greek style he waves them on and doesn't give a damn. Occasionally he picks up the CB and shouts down it, we don't understand what he is saying but we get the gist.

*

Noticing the others stirring I take my chance. Today is the day. The sun is showing her full strength, the day is breaking in full glow. Shards of light hit the rocks. The others are rubbing their eyes and sitting up.

I'm going I say.

They look at me, for a moment perplexed.

I motion to the diving board at the other end of the beach. At some point it has been partly destroyed and now all that remains is a concrete plinth sticking out of the side of the cliff with metal rods poking out of the end. I want to say it is thirty feet high but I couldn't tell you for sure. The boys have spent the whole day before diving off it. They show off taking more daring leaps each time, sprinting back up the cliff path for another turn. I want to join them. They fob me off with:

Don't worry little Emz – you're only small.

I am small. I am determined. Before the others have barely left their sleeping bags I have stripped off the dress to my bikini, which I am also still wearing from the day before.

Where you going Emz?

I look at the diving board.

Wait, wait a minute.

I am gone walking steadily across the beach and up the steps carved into the cliff. Through the scrub and prickly pears with graffiti carved into their leaves. The soles of my feet scuff the gritty track; the skin is hard from six weeks without shoes and only battered leather sandals when we travel. By the time I reach the top the others are running after me, young athletic figures cutting through the cliff side to my rescue. When they reach the top I am striding along the diving board.

Wait!

I reach the end. I hear my name whistle through the air as I launch myself from the top. I will not be outdone by the boys even if they are older than me. The world swooshes past in blue and white. The shock of the water hits my feet and swallows me whole, shooting into my nostrils and filling my mouth. My bikini top is around my neck, the bottoms are almost there too. When I surface, gurgling and laughing, the boys are running down the cliff as fast as they can to haul me out. They are looking shocked but are laughing too. Jan, the eldest boy, throws his hand towards me, but wait, before I swim to the shore to take his hand, let's dive deeper. I want to explain how I came to be sleeping on a beach in Greece aged eleven.

Emma McKenzie

Cailleach

Fog hangs light on the air around me, a thin veil draped softly over the mountain peaks, faint flecks of water dancing over my naked skin. My breath forms miniature clouds in front of my eyes distorting my vision and sending the world into a kaleidoscope of greens and browns and blues. My altitude provides a vantage over a beautifully uninhabited peninsula. A thought whispers that perhaps I am entirely alone in the world. I stand perfectly naked and uncaring. A breeze tickles the tips of my long hair across my hips yet does not chill me. Unbound from the material world I am gifted a special closeness with the natural, a mutually beneficial relationship. All was calm and still. Alas, in the furthest corner of my mind, almost not there at all and yet unmistakable, a quiver of anxiety. Something, somewhere, was unequivocally wrong.

The stillness was politely interrupted by a tiny song thrush fluttering from the sky and landing on the peak of a jutting rock a few paces in front of me. He hopped around for a moment until he was comfortably settled, and then lay his gaze on me and proceeded to open his beak to release his chorus. His tiny chest pulsated with rhythm but the sound I heard was not bird song. The air around was completely undisturbed by noise, instead isolated in my head came a steady, echoing heartbeat. I watched the little bird, seemingly engaged in a lengthy melody, become more ecstatic and almost violent in his performance. And as he does so the heartbeat increases both in pace and volume. He jumps up and down on the spot, wings flapping furiously. I notice a distinct lack of breath clouds in my vision and become suddenly aware of an icy wing stinging my extremities, my nipples hardening against the chill. I move to try and cover my naked body with my arms to a realisation that I cannot move.

And so instead I stand alone, petrified and unbreathing, the previously faint sliver of anxiety building behind my eyes and leaking into my stomach, churning up bile and forcing it burning into my throat. My body lurches forward to release the vomit, choking up the contents of my stomach and yet I cannot part my lips, so the vomit fills my mouth and nose, threatening to suffocate me. My head begins to pound from the building pressure. I strive to open my mouth, to be sick, to scream, to call for help but to no avail. Instead my nose begins to leak the burning fluid and a stream of tears runs from unblinking eyes, the pressure in my skull never lessening in its rise. The song thrush has ceased to perform and now he stands watching me, head tilted to one side in an observation of morbid curiosity. The warmth and thickness of the liquid escaping my eyes strikes fear within me. A burning sting at my tear ducts confirms that it is not tears I am crying but blood, and the world turns red.

A high-pitched ringing starts up in my ears, my heartbeat slow as I strain to no avail to release the bile filling my mouth, choking me. As I desperately attempt to breathe once more. The red tinted world begins to fizz and falter. My legs are rendered useless and I fall to my knees.

I am dying. The thought nothing more than a ripple as it reaches the surface of my mind. Just as the world begins to turn black, the ringing in my ears becomes piercing and rhythmic and as my body falls to the grass, limp and lifeless, I am no longer in a deserted peninsula.

I awoke, gasping, desperately trying to remember how to breathe, the bed beneath me sodden with sweat. I wiped a drop of blood from my nose before it fell onto my green, paisley bedding. And something caught in my throat which could have been the start of a laugh.

Outside the sun was blaring, the skies perfectly blue, trees unmoving. Yet I could still feel the moist air caressing my skin, still had the scent of country air clutching to my nostrils, and a feel of dread sitting in the pit of my stomach.

Emma McNicholas

Reaper

Fifty Fifie herring boat drifters,
full mizzenmast sheets windward side,
launch out from Wick one Lammas tide.
One, the Reaper, leads the fleet.
Crew of four, young and callow,
smoking cigarettes, setting nets;
wet whispers of forgotten kisses
and absent sisters.

Log line five, then ten.
From sonorous sea,
a hundred cran of herring.
Worth fifty on the quay.

Dusk at Duncansby Head –
wind turns northward.
Skipper calls steady lads, yawp aboon.
Northern Nanny will arrive afore moon.

Beyond the rupestral stacks,
gulls and storm petrel make for land –
a sign of mighty storm to come.
Shouts to make for home.

Reaper's skipper protests
that beneath these crests
lie rotted wombs of fishy flesh;
sailors' tombs at Poseidon's altar.
The fleet must weather the storm –
harbour is empty on falling tide:
all to head for Dunbeath cove!

But his words are lost in hues and cries.

From Spitsbergen to Iceland,
now down these merciless shores,
Nanny whips, caresses and spurns
the fleet like a haunted lover –
mocking that for which she yearns.

One by one, the boats shudder,
falter and spoil. Crash against the harbour.
For Reaper, adrift hundred cables north,
blankets of dense grey air
drive over her stern.
Jump over bow and groyne.

Yet she runs her briny gauntlet.
Lurches in thirty foot waves
until safely beneath stilted cliffs of Dunbeath –
where she swamps upon the beach.

Rupert Nevin

Vitality

You hold a gleaming peacock;
your nails clean and short,
its claw to your claw
is scaled and dead.
You look away
from the obscenity;
its gold, yellow, red plumes
match your pristine jerkin
and the sheen of your eyes.
Your rough timber table
displays the bloody feast
of limp swan, deer, hare and pig,
protruding luminous bones
of furred and feathered once-life
that lingers
in black peppercorn eyes,
earth – walked hooves
and the yearning
of the canine.

B. T. Oldfield

Elisa Day

Lion fur spirals down porcelain skin,
her beauty snatched from Aphrodite.
Words mingle in the air,
venomous poison begins to seep.

First day, a stuttering tango of words,
candlelit chase commences.
Sweaty palms find solace,
Jaws of metal inch closer to flesh.

Second day, single rose presented,
vibrant beauties kiss her fingertips.
Frail stem held steady in controlling hands,
twisted sickly paper petals left behind.

Third day, crimson and flesh connecting
stage set amongst the old oak, restrained.
Lover's secret embrace,
red veins imprinting the soil.

Send her away with a rose,
may she go into the night.
Her beauty was too potent,
may she go into the light.

Mathew Payne

The Lost Legions

In the past twenty years, the deaths of thousands of Italian soldiers in the Russian campaign during the Second World War have gradually disappeared from history books in primary and secondary schools. It is not a case that the process began just after the end of the First Republic and the advent of Berlusconism. With all its flaws, the First Republic was always careful to retain the fear of Fascism at the centre of Italian political agenda. The Italian constitution itself and the men who sat down in 1946 to write it down, established as one of the principles of the Republic that the 'apology of Fascism' should be punished as a crime. The Second Republic started off winking at organised crime and using different ways of giving new life to extreme-right thinking.

The subtle revisionist project of rehabilitating Fascism includes deleting from official history all the battles in which Mussolini sent Italian soldiers to die a less then heroic death. For instance, Italian children who started school from the late 1990s onwards never read or studied that almost 100,000 Italian soldiers died in the Russian Campaign because they were sent to fight at polar temperatures in their summer uniforms, ill-equipped and ill-trained.

The involvement of Italian troops in the Russian campaign was due more to political than to military causes. Just after the beginning of the German attack on Russia, Mussolini asked Hitler if he could send an Italian expeditionary force to the Russian front, with the intention of demonstrating to the Furher the strength of the Fascist troops and their loyalty to Nazi Germany. It was, therefore, a purely symbolic gesture, and, as so often happens with emotional impulses, it was destined to end in disaster.

The Italian Expeditionary Force (CSIR) started to move into the battle area on July 1941. It consisted of 60,000 men, and was sent to the southern part of the front, attached to the German XI Army. Even in this first phase, lack of transport forced the Italian troops to carry out exhausting marches over the muddy Ukrainian roads.

17TH AUGUST 1941, 5PM

It's our second week of trekking across what we think is Ukraine. We should be reaching the Don Front in around two weeks, if we haven't totally lost our way. My men marched the whole day carrying their heavy packs and their low moods. These boys are ordinary folk: peasant farmers, shoemakers, bakers, iron workers. They are the working class which Fascism promised to protect. I have received precise orders of avoiding contact with the enemy, but I can see that the men feel closer to the Ukrainian peasants we encounter on our way than to the Fascist elite who sent them here in their summer uniforms. Ukrainian summer consists of blistering heat in the days and very cold nights, with a temperature excursion of around 20 degrees Celsius between day and night. It feels like an ironic reminder of the fact that we were supposed to fight in Africa. The dust cloud that rises from our tracks while we march reminds me of Africa, too. It mixes with our sweat as we advance and by evening we are unrecognisable. We always arrive dead tired and the boys have to fix something to eat. One of them goes to search for a cabbage, another for a tomato, the luckier ones captured a chicken during the trek. The local children have learned a few words of Italian. They shout VIVA ITALIA, DARE ACQUA, DARE PASTA, when they see us. They are so nice to us and so amusing that I can't deny the men to interact with them. We try to do everything we can to please them. In exchange they give us the gift of a few moments of family life, which we already miss. I allow my men to fraternise with the enemy, as I can hardly see these children as the enemy, and I can hardly deny my men their share of human contact, after having marched through fields of rye and sunflowers for days, without ever seeing a living soul, apart from themselves.

Lieutenant Corti

15TH DECEMBER 1942, 8PM

We kept walking, even when the night came on. It's cold, colder than ever. Our breath freezes on our beards, and we walk on, in silence. We look ahead and there is nothing: no trees, no houses, no people. There is only us and the endless snow. I think about lying down on the snow and closing my eyes. Will that be my death? How many of my men behind are having the same thought and throwing themselves down on the snow to never get up again? I can't stop to check on them, I know I am losing them, but I need to bring the survivors to safety. I am frightened of getting frost-bite, but I walk on. We are like shadows, the Italian ghost army disappearing in the snow. A strong cold wind blows up and we're all white. What day is today? On we walk, every step in the snow is one less to reach home. The sun rises and the whiteness of the snow together with the sunlight dazzles us. I don't know what to think or what I'm doing anymore. Every now and then I hold my breath and I think … now, I'll die. But I don't, and I walk on. I eat handfuls of snow to try and keep my mouth hydrated in some way. We walked along steadily but slowly, even by forcing myself I couldn't proceed any faster. I kept repeating to myself now is the time I will die, and the thought went along with each step. The cold is torturing my body and my mind … I am lost, I turn to look if the men are still following. There is less than twenty of us now. I collect all my strength and I shout … Come on, follow me, there is a train waiting for us somewhere. A train back home.

Lieutenant Corti

Lieutenant Corti was captured by the Red Army on the 18th December 1942 and taken to a prison camp in Siberia. This was the worst time for POW in Russia: after the victory of Stalingrad the Red Army was overwhelmed by the huge number of prisoners and the resources were stretched to the limit. The majority of prisoners captured in the end of 1942 and the beginning of 1943 died in the early part of 1943. Thousands died of cold, hunger, typhus and other diseases connected to malnutrition. Lieutenant Corti survived and in September 1945 he was among 1700 generals, officials, soldiers, and civilians who were the first to be repatriated to Italy. By November 1946, 10,032 men were returned to Italy, and the Soviets declared the process complete, leaving unaccounted for 60,000 others. Only in the 1990's, formal evidence was produced of 64,500 Italians captured alive by the Soviets, 38,000 of whom had officially died in prison camps, while the remaining 16,468 were declared missing.

Nicoletta Peddis

I Counted to Eleven

A makeshift heart rate monitor sat in the corner of the dining room showing four names: 'Adam', 'Maria', 'Morgan' and 'Simon', all four of which had stable rhythm as the line moved from left to right. A single lightbulb shone down on the dining table where four people sat.

Each placemat had plastic knives and forks on either side of paper plates. The table was a dark wood colour with a multitude of darker stains across its top, a golden trim decorating the edge and no tablecloth covering it. Each of the four dining chairs seated one of the four people named on the heart monitor. Adam in one seat, Simon to his right, Maria to Simon's right and Morgan to Maria's right. The door into the dining room opened and a figure slunk in.

'How are my guests doing today?' The Bony Man asked, bending down and staring directly into Simon's eyes, causing him to flinch away. 'Oh, this won't do. Your plug has come loose and your hair is a mess.' The Bony man forced Simon's head forward, revealing an electrical plug jammed into the back of his neck. He forced the plug further into Simon's neck, causing him to stifle a scream and the beeping on the heart rate monitor to increase, he then proceeded to push Simon back against the chair, with a brittle-looking hand, and brush the blond hair, that was clung to his face, back. 'At least all of your arm bands are still tight.' The Bony Man sighed as he floated over and tapped the heart rate monitor. 'You're all still with me,' he turned back to the dining table, 'that's wonderful – because it's dinner time!'

'Why are you doing this?' Maria cried, she had red streaks down her cheeks and her brown hair was clumped together. As she spoke, Adam looked over to Simon and the two made eye contact, as if Adam was asking if he was okay.

'I'm just being a good host, my dear.' He clapped his hands together as he walked over to her chair, placing his hands on her shoulders. 'Something that is frightfully lacking these days. Do you know how many parties I've attended where the host makes no effort? Too many! I'm feeding you, am I not? And I have you all hooked up to that monitor over there, just to make sure that you all remain in good health while you're here.' He stood back up and pointed to the monitor. 'Look! No flatlines! There aren't any problems.'

'Aren't any – what is wrong with you?!' Maria began to raise her voice. Morgan began to quietly weep next to her and Adam sunk down in his chair, wincing at the plug in his neck shifting, before looking back at Simon, who had closed his eyes.

'Nothing!' The Bony Man slammed his hands on the table between Maria and Morgan. 'It's you! People. Like. You.' He picked up one of the knives and quickly stabbed it into the back of her right hand. 'No. Don't scream anymore. You're ruining the party for everyone else and anger won't solve anything.' He forced a smile back across his face. 'Besides, I said it's dinner time.' Maria stifled cries with the knife still in her hand.

Simon opened his eyes and looked at Adam, who was still looking at him. Adam looked down to his right hand and then back up at Simon to suggest that he look at the metal restraints over his wrists, holding him in place and on the chair. Adam had already managed loosen the restraints around his legs from hours of small movements against them, enough to the point he would be able to pull them off if his hands were free. Simon's eyes moved down to Adam's restraints and while The Bony Man scolded Maria, Adam slowly moved his right hand, showing Simon how loose the restraints were.

'I have no time for insolence.' The Bony Man said, tugging on a hem on his suit. He floated over to the heart rate monitor and pressed down one of four, large buttons. At the table Morgan began to shake, an electric jolt fired through the plug and into her neck. Before she had time to scream her body flopped down onto the table and the line by her name on the monitor turned flat, adding a single shrill tone to the beeping. 'Whoopsie, wrong one.' The Bony Man chuckled before turning back to the buttons. 'I thought that was Maria's,' he whispered to himself, 'so it's either to the left or right of that one.'

Adam and Simon looked into each other's eyes. Maria let out the cries she was previously stifling. Adam mouthed the words 'I love you' to Simon as The Bony Man said, 'this one,' from the other side of the room. Moments after he spoke Maria met the same fate as Morgan, the same jolt to the neck, the same flopping onto the table and the same flatline added to the noise.

'There we go!' He said, twirling, facing back towards Adam and Simon. 'Well, hopefully we shouldn't have to lose anymore guests, should we?' He paused for a moment. 'Perhaps we should find some new guests soon.' He walked to the space between Adam and Simon and bent down. A thin layer of sweat began to form on Adam's forehead. 'Now, if you lovebirds will behave, we can have dinner. Does that sound good?' He looked between the two.

'Yes.' Adam said finally. 'It sounds good.' He spoke in a flat tone.

'Well isn't that wonderful!' The Bony Man shot back up and made for the door, turning back to the table before leaving. 'Don't go anywhere! Dinner is on its way.' He crept out, closing the door behind him.

Waiting for the click of the door to close felt longer to Adam than all of the events he had just witnessed. Once he heard the click, he counted to five and tensed his right arm, causing the restraint to crack open – freeing his hand. He let out a sigh of relief and smiled for the first time when he looked at Simon.

'You might not want to watch this, Si.' He said, grasping the plug in the back of his neck and yanking it out without hesitation. His face turned red as he stifled as much noise as he could as a third flat tone added, leaving only Simon's heart rate. The rest of the restraints and monitors stuck to his chest came off easily for both himself and Simon. 'Simon, I love you, but I hope this is the most I ever hurt you.' Before Simon got the chance to respond the plug was yanked out of his neck and the rest of his restraints and monitors removed.

Simon wasted no time in standing up and pulling Adam into a hug.

'Christ, let's go.' He said to Adam, taking his hand and making for the door.

Simon reached for the door knob, only to have the entire door move out of his reach, revealing a figure in the doorway.

'Crap!'

Matthew Pickering

Blackout

Rhonda was sitting at the kitchen table, her fingers resting on her temples. She could feel them pulsating. My god, what a splitting headache! Never in her life had her head pounded like this. It felt as if someone had beaten her with a baseball bat all night.

She groaned while rubbing her temples. Never mind the baseball bat, now it feels like she had been hit by a truck. Rhonda rose from her chair, but immediately fell back down on it and started rocking back and forth. Her pain was too intense. She didn't feel like making breakfast so she just left a box of cereal on the table with a carton of milk and an empty bowl right next to it. She didn't plan on eating anything because of her intense nausea. The breakfast was supposed to be for Timothy who had not come downstairs yet.

'Timmy,' Rhonda yelled 'Breakfast!'

No one came. Usually Timothy would come sprinting downstairs, excited for breakfast. However, she could not hear any signs of him coming.

Rhonda didn't think much of it. All she could think about was not throwing up. She started to take slow, deep breaths to relieve the nausea.

'Don't get sick, don't get sick,' she kept chanting to herself in her mind, the last thing she wanted to do was clean up the floor, especially in her current state.

'Timmy!' she yelled louder, not sure if he could hear her.

Eventually the little blond boy came in the kitchen, slower than usual. His intense blue eyes captured the floor. His gaze avoiding Rhonda's when he sat down as he poured the cereal in his bowl. He ate slowly not saying a word. She was puzzled by his silence. Normally Timothy was a very talkative child. Feeling uncomfortable, Rhonda decided to start a conversation.

'How was school yesterday? I don't remember you telling me.' Timothy was chewing the cereal slowly as if thinking hard about something; eventually he swallowed and answered in a quiet voice:

'Fine.'

'I wish work was fine,' Rhonda said, while rubbing her pounding head 'I had an absolute rubbish day.' Timothy nodded, got up from his chair and was heading towards the door with his backpack, as if he was in a hurry.

'Honey, where are you going?'

'School,' he answered quickly.

'But school doesn't start for another half hour, and you haven't eaten any breakfast.'

'I will eat when I get there,' he spoke almost too quickly for her to understand him. Now, she could no longer take this. She got up and approached him, ignoring the pain in her head.

'Timothy, I am not feeling well right now, please tell me what is wrong.' The minute she got a hold of his arm, he flinched from her. He looked at her directly in her eyes for the first time this morning and he looked terrified. His breathing was rapid and his tiny frame was shaking. Rhonda then noticed a dark purple bruise on his upper arm; it looked like the shape of a hand.

'Oh, my baby!' she cried, horrified. 'Who did this to you?' Timothy ran out of the house without giving her an answer. Rhonda was furious. Who hurt her little boy? She grabbed his unfinished bowl of cereal and headed towards the sink. Maybe it was his father. From what she remembered during their marriage he had never been patient with her or Timothy. She would call him on the phone and confront him about it when she finished the dishes. Just when she reached the sink, she could smell this strong, yet familiar smell. She dropped the bowl causing it to shatter, when she stared in horror at the sink, in which several empty bottles of Domaine des Rêves Brisés were strewn. Suddenly, the memories from last night came flooding to her. What had she done? Tears came down her cheeks. No, no, no, no… No wonder Timothy was avoiding eye contact with her.

He was scared of her… again.

Elisabeth Prestgard

Chaos in the Improv

Chaos in the improv
Hard to follow from an outsider's point of view.
Men in drag giving laughs,
delighting the ladies.
A hilarious thought
ladies lying on laps,
leaving behind all inhibitions,
where nothing is taboo.
Constant chatter,
wondering what the neighbours think
of the daily antics.
Never the same
from day to day.
How good it is to be different.

Laura Russell

Stays time

A sea of white lining up
to see the Master,
in his yellow banyan.
A pineapple pattern with parrots,
gracefully draped over the body,
hiding the Master's modesty.

The queue goes down quickly,
as laces get tightened,
stomachs shrink
and waists nipped in.
Busoms get heightened,
pulled, prodded and poked.

All assemble near
a sweeping settee,
the ladies leering and leaning,
at the stays Master.
While he is proud of his work
Ready for the next day.

Laura Russell

1947

The child stands at the bedroom window. It is morning but the sky is still a dark bruise. She is cold in her nightie and bare feet but it is a familiar state now. The delight at watching her own and her mother's breath escape in plumes of vapour has long since lost its novelty. They are no longer dragons.

'You'll never believe it,' says her mother, struggling to hoist the sash window upwards. With two more shoves, it reluctantly opens its mouth. 'Look how high the snow is, Anne.'

Her mother drops to her knees and takes the small chubby hand, placing it onto a bank of rough ice just beneath the ledge. It is a conjuror's trick, an impossibility. It is biblical. Overnight, a tidal wave of frozen water has risen the height of a house and settled itself like a discomforting blanket all around them.

The child pats the top of the drift and smiles – for this is the reaction she feels her mother is looking for – and the cold hurts her teeth. The whiteness is blinding to her sleepy eyes, the silence is eerie. No sound vibrates, as though they are in a vacuum.

'Could we walk along the top of it?' she asks. Her mother laughs.

'I don't think so darling, best not risk it.'

A blast of icy wind blows into the room. It scours the inside of her nostrils and makes her chest ache. The window is closed. It is winter 1947 and they would never see snow like it ever again.

Anne finds her grandmother sitting downstairs beside a meagre fire, enrobed in several blankets and wearing a knitted hat. Despite all this she still maintains an imperious air; straight-backed, mouth set, as though this is entirely appropriate garb for a woman of her age and standing. She turns her head to indicate the nearby teapot.

Pulling herself up to her full height beside the table, Anne solemnly handles the task as instructed and pours the old woman a cup. Steam issues from the brown liquid.

'Has the snow swallowed us whole Grandmama?' she asks. She is drawn onto the old woman's lap and they both look window-ward at the whiteout beyond.

'Now you listen to me, I've lived in this house a long time and it's weathered worse storms than this. Winter doesn't last forever and when it's over you'll forget it was so bad.'

'Will we go back home then?'

Her mother walks into the room, catching the tail of this conversation and the two women exchange a look over the top of the small, brown head. She takes the poker and begins to stab at the fire.

'We mustn't let this go out.'

'Won't daddy be cold in the old house all by himself?'

Her mother tenses and stares into the coals. 'From now on we're not going to talk about your father. Is that clear?' She steadies herself against the chimney breast with one hand, brandishing the poker in the other. The tip of it quivers, like the note in her voice, before she shoves it back into the coal scuttle. Anne looks at Grandmama who dismisses her with a wink. As she wanders off to the pantry in search of food she hears her mother weeping. It is a familiar sound now that no longer provokes alarm but rather a mild interest.

'What ever shall I do?'

It is one of her mother's favourite phrases, the emphasis always on the word 'ever' she notes, as her jaw slowly works around the molten biscuit in her mouth.

'You did the right thing,' soothes the older woman in a cut-glass voice, which has softened a little over the years. 'The only thing. It wasn't safe for you in that house.'

Why wasn't it safe, wonders Anne. Was the house harbouring some ill spirit, a monster in the attic? Or was it unsafe like holding a pair of scissors the wrong way? Or not testing the bath water with an elbow before her baby brother is lowered in, his legs drawing up to his chest and his fists angrily grabbing at the air? What could possibly have been so dangerous that meant they could not stay but had to flee one morning, before the sky had properly given way to the cold grey fog of the day?

Anne finds the thought unsettling. She has to force the last of the biscuit's gritty syrup down past her throat with effort. In the end, she decides it must be something to do with the snow.

Mummy must have heard the weather forecast and realised their house wasn't strong enough. Perhaps it had been made of straw or wood. Like those in the story with the pigs. That's why they had to run away to Grandmama's, before this icy wind blew them all down.

Kathryn Sharman

Signs of Rain

I fell in love with her at 12.19pm. I was turned down by 3 o'clock. Love is a funny thing. Oh the mountains we have to climb. The mountain may not like this at times, but it will come around eventually. She teaches Drama from what I am told. Though most say you can walk all over her without even meaning to. Walking over her is not my intention. I have been warned that her husband left her for another woman. I didn't take it as a warning, more like a justification for my companionship. In the mornings, she liked to eat alone in the studio sipping from a thermos. In the nights, she hears her roommate having sex with her sister's boyfriend. In the afternoons she pretends that she is Julie Andrews. When I brought her a copy of a DVD and insisted we watch it together she told me I was very sweet but she couldn't spend time with me outside of school. Now she spends time with me without really ever knowing it. I like to think she knows though. Out the moulding window I see a storm cooking and yet inside this room it is the illusion of calm. Except for one single droplet that mixes into a thermos. It tasted of saline and malt.

Benjamin Shaw

October 11th 1988 (A Figure Emerges from the Proverbial Closet)

no more hiding in shadows. the clandestine meetings after sunset
no more sneaking a surreptitious glance at parties
or feelings of trepidation 'cause you held their hand
exquisite hand – artists hand.
in public view

break from their chains of bigotry.
of judgement. be free to;
love without apologising
kiss without a filter: now
sashay down that city sidewalk henny
you ethereal creature
                                      of candescence and creation.

Joe Shaw

ignorance equals fear equals silence equals death

instead of checking for monsters
the ones from nightmares
that lurk under children's beds
we now look for dirty,
aids-ridden

gays

infecting hard-working christian americans
through promiscuity and sex
they've taken our cinemas,
covering the seats in contaminated ejaculate
the public parks
where we walk our labradors
orgies in seedy clubs, concocting a mixture of
disease and scum

14,000
1989
this will only rise. trust me, i'm from the future

three wise monkeys
though wise they are not
one covers his eyes, blind,
blind to the hospital bed, now empty because of a dilatory diagnosis
one covers his ears, deaf,
deaf to the words of frightened youth, who are irresolute and lost
one covers his mouth, silent, scared of judgement, of exile, of
   quarantine

rip off that pink triangle, stapled to your flannel shirt
for decades too long.
for it is not a badge of stigma anymore
don't hide in the closet again, baby you've been there
it's dark and cold and you are not
the equation must be reformed
knowledge equals trust equals conversation equals survival

you are not dirty, not decaying
you are effervescent, honey
you are fabulous
and you will live
a long and happy life

Joe Shaw

He Who Stole Me Away

I was born on a Tuesday.

Premature. Seven weeks and five days early.
Mum fell down the stairs; that's what triggered me.
I got an infection after three days,
but I beat it.

Mum came and sat with me every day
when I was sick.
She would read to me from the newspaper,
all the happy stories.

He was there when I came home
for the first time.
I can't remember what home smelled like
back then, but I'm not sure you're supposed to.

I was shown a video
of myself learning how to walk.
I scraped my arms on the wood floors.
I kept going.

I took my first steps when I turned one.
Mum was so proud of me, and
he was there as well.
I wonder if he was proud of me too?

I saw him on TV once, saw pictures of
how they came for him
and stole him away from us.
They let him go after a while.

He came home, and I
was sat playing with Mum's keys.
I didn't realise he had been gone.
I barely knew him at all.

But I was happy. I remember
drawing a picture with my Mum
in the kitchen. I drew a dog because I wanted one.
We didn't get a dog.

He used to yell at her – at Mum.
The house used to smell funny, but not
in a good way. He would get angry
if the smell started to fade away.

Mum wasn't the same after the shouting was over.
She would hide her face from me
and she wouldn't draw with me anymore.
We wouldn't do anything anymore.

I never got angry at him, though, like
he did with me. I would follow Mum's example
and hide away from him – not look him in the eye.
I remember the day I couldn't wake her up.

They came back for him then,
snapped shiny bracelets on his wrists, and
he said bad words to them.
I hid under Mum's bed and I was left alone.

He came back, his footsteps loud and
his hands shaking.
He said we had to leave home,
but I didn't want to go.

People had already taken Mum away,
but that didn't mean that I wanted to go.
I barely knew him.
I remember how big his hands were, though.

I died on a Tuesday.

Megan Shield

The Giant's Gold

A crying child abandoned at the maw of the cave, dripping stalactites jutting from the ceiling; a slavering jaw to eat any tendrils of light that attempted to infiltrate. It bit down on her, swallowed her whole and left no remains.

The beast unfurled itself, releasing a shuddering breath that set the metallic floor rattling, its reptilian tail sweeping an arc of brilliant, shining gold to the side as it rose. The snout of the creature was almost the size of the child standing before it. It was not dark in the open cavern, the gaps in the rock above just enough for the pale light of the morning to creep in, reflecting off the treasured gold that lay beneath the beast. It cast itself against the surrounding stone, flickering in defiance at the shadow that strove to cross the threshold of the creature's den. The beast looked at the child. 'I will look after you,' it said, voice smooth and clear.

The beast taught the child to read and write, it taught her how to hunt and gather. The beast raised the child with great care and as much affection as the noble creature could give to the small human. Soon the child was taller than the beast's snout. Now a woman, she could fend for herself, survive by herself. The time she spent inside the cave with the giant she considered a parent grew less, but the beast did not mind. She was bound to the earth by mortal chains, even as she beat against them. After all, it was the involuntary desire for immortality that instinctively drove humanity to explore. That same unrelenting search and unfading desire was the pinnacle of what made them human. The beast had never had to long for time, content in spending its endless days within the confines of the glittering home.

The woman had not returned in a week, choosing instead to cross the land farther than she'd been on her own before. Wild; cold; still. The woods at the precipice of Winter's chill was a barren place, the ground crunching softly beneath her feet as she admired the hoarfrost coating the lifeless vegetation around her. The sun began lowering itself, taking with it the last dregs of warmth the day had offered. She was nearing the edge of the forest when she stopped, watching a bright flame from a distance as it swayed against the breeze that threatened to blow it out – a candle lit beside the door of a home. Out of necessity and curiosity, she found herself walking towards it.

She had not seen another human in many years, barely remembered her life before the beast had taken her in. He was older than her, silver beginning to line his head and chin, and taller. He towered above her as he stood guarding the entrance to the home, and upon seeing her, something lighted in his eyes. He greeted her with a rough accent, moving aside to allow her in. The fire was lit, the warmth spreading around the small space. He offered her food and a bed for the night. He offered her a drink that tingled on her tongue. She was not tired and instead found herself talking with the stranger long after the sun had disappeared. With only the flame as a light, her mind swam dizzy with the questions he asked, and she found herself enjoying the human company. She spoke of the beast who raised her, glad to have someone with whom she could share her pride and love for the beast, who would also know of the creature's kindness and generosity. He spoke of the farmland he kept, the town he lived near. It had been hard to understand him at first, his words shortened, clipped, but she soon found herself leaning into the voice, listening intently. And when they had finished eating, when they had placed their empty cups onto the table, she had let him lead her to bed.

When she awoke the next morning – her hands grappling for the covers to warm her bare body against the cold – she looked down at the man beside her, still comfortable in sleep. He was still asleep when she left, leaving him a note telling him she would return and a gold coin that the beast told her to carry should she need to stop somewhere for the night. It took her another week before she returned home, the unlit cave more comforting than the fire-warmed house of the man. The beast welcomed her, teeth bared, longer and sharper than some of the stalactites. The most human expression it could make, a smile. Two days passed, she spoke to the beast of the man she met, the time she had spent away. The beast listened intently, as it always did. It didn't comment when she told it she would be going back soon, it had never denied her any freedom, only offering understanding. But on that third morning, they were awoken. The earth rattling underneath them. Just as it had done the first day she had arrived here, the beast unfurled and shifted, rising to its full height. It once more bared its teeth. Only, this time, there was no welcoming grin. There was no shuddering breath. Only the calm movements of a large predator. 'What is it?' she asked the beast. Already moving towards the direction of the noise. With every step the sound got louder, no longer just a rumble of the Earth but a chanting that pierced the air around them. The beast remained silent, remained still, and she did not look at it as she made her way from the heart of the cave.

They stood along the horizon, blotting out the sun. The only sign that it was there was the red that cut across the sky like a wound weeping. If the beast was the stalactites hovering along the cave ceiling, these were the jutting stalagmites that pierced the ground beneath. They stood, hundreds of men, penetrating the land with their incessant march towards them. They were coming towards the cave. She looked back at the beast, its eyes focused on the crowd; leading the force was a tall man with greying hair, in his hand was a gold coin. She understood then, what it was. The terrible thing that had woken them both, the great and fearsome monster that ravaged the land and its resources. She understood what it wanted: the treasure it had learned was hidden here. 'I know what it is now,' she told her protector.

Leaving her only family behind her, she walked to meet the amassing army. They stopped, metres away from each other. Her clothes began to burn, the smell of smoke filling the air. Her hair became ash, her lungs became fire. She did not care now that she was bare before them, did not reach for anything to cover herself with. Not as her skin became scales. She released a breath, smoke curling in the air before her, a deep, shuddering breath she had heard so many times before. A breath of something beautiful, immortal and wild.

A. L. Smith

Days of the Week

No one likes Monday. It's not really his fault. He's the eldest, the busiest, the most organized, yet he still can't remember what's going on. He always wears a suit, perfectly ironed, with not a button out of place. People dread to see him coming.

Tuesday has been labelled dull and boring. She never has anything to look forward to, stuck in a strange limbo of not being at the start of something, yet being nowhere near the end either. She looks out at the sky, taking in the shapes of the clouds, the changing colours as the sun rises and falls, all the while wishing to disappear into it.

Wednesday is always in the middle of everything. Things are either going perfectly or terribly for him, determining his stress level. Either way he's not very optimistic for the future.

The most overlooked is Thursday. She is quiet, peaceful, happy. While not the most out-spoken she sure is the most ambitious, thinking about the future and how things can affect everyone, even if she is ignored most of the time.

The centre of attention is Friday. Everyone looks forward to his arrival and he knows it, chatting happily to anyone who will listen. He looks casual, with jeans and a hand run through his hair. He'd give you the shirt off his back to make you happy, but you'd never ask for it because his presence is enough.

No one sees Saturday in the mornings. She's either sleeping or has already been out of the house for hours. She works hard and plays hard, doing chores or errands before meeting with friends to go out. She is rarely seen without a drink in her hand and can befriend even the grumpiest of people.

And lastly, we have Sunday, the youngest and surprisingly the calmest. Some call him lazy, but it's rather more of a content satisfaction – nothing can change now so he accepts things and tried to be happy with them. If not, he will strive to be better when things reset. He has a way of relaxing you without doing much. That is until it grows dark and he introduces you to his older brother again.

Emily Smith

The Noise They Make

The air has been dark for a while now. The sky, dust. It drifts to the ground and settles. You are alone. Your boots are thick with it. It squelches as you walk. You have walked far from where you began. Home is distant now. You try not to think about it.

There used to be noise in the trees. They used to move and talk to each other. They once had colour, and you are sure that you used to be able to see the tops. There is an ache in your legs. How long has that been there? Why are they sticky? You can't lower your eyes to check. They strain with the effort. Focus only on the path ahead.

If that is a path. You've been following it for some time. You have to reach the end. You must. At the end there will be answers. There are no noises here. Nothing but the whispers. Distant whispers far away. Far among the trees. Then in your ear. But there is no breath. You do not turn around. The end is where they told you to go. They said, back then. Back then. Back when the trees had colour and made noises and the ground didn't throb and send tremors up your bones. You don't know what colour they were. How could you have forgotten what colour they were? There is no colour here.

There is a ringing. You think it's in your ears. Your fingertips are swollen from swinging by your sides and your hands are heavy as you raise them to your head. There is something smeared on them. It gets on your ears as you push your palms against them. It mutes the noise. Like music through walls. You do not stop walking. You let your arms go limp. They creak with the motion. The ringing continues. The pitch gets higher. You do not stop walking. It gets louder. You do not stop walking. It is uncomfortable. Piercing your ears. Filling your head. Wailing and screaming and reaching into the corners of your consciousness until there is no room left for anything else. The pitch is too high for you to hear yet you feel it vibrate on every inch of your skin.

It speaks to you. There is meaning hiding behind the noise. When it is loud enough and you strain your ears enough and you hold your breath you can make out words. A thousand voices whispering and shouting all at once:

DO NOT BE AFRAID

You are not. The trees are silent. With every step your boots sink into the ground deeper and deeper. Your clothes are wet but you feel no cold. You don't feel anything at all.

The path ends. The air goes black.

Rachel Smith

Unkindness

A late October mist began to settle across the moors, seizing the landscape as the full moon, glorious and radiant, rose from in between the trees bare of foliage out in the horizon.

The fireflies danced, basking in the evening autumn air. They formed constellations in the thickening fog. There were no words carried along the breeze, not a sound – only winter's looming chill. Iridescent eyes darting from behind the decaying trees, beneath the cover of the shadows cast, yet all remain in peace.

Tranquillity could not last – it never does.

Echoing, a rumbling howl forced its way throughout the moors. Ravens took to the skies, calling warnings to their unkindness.

A couple of miles east, passed several hundred trees the fog had not yet reached a broken-down car. Instead the air was filled with smoke, emanating from the car; only the headlight could pierce its veil.

It was far from silent here, the night was filled with mechanical hisses and profanity from Shane. He had torn through the skin on his palm while trying to repair his car. His blood dripped from the gash in his hand.

The unkindness of ravens flew overhead, screeching through the skies. The sound clawed its way through Shane's head, the volume forced him to recoil. With them came the fog, quickly descending on Shane. His headlights became unable to carve out his surroundings; as time pressed on they were slowly diming with the battery of his car.

The moors raged back at his anger, echoing with his own words – along with the vigorous rustling of leaves and what sounded like the snapping of bones. Shane's ears clung to the sound of the disturbed undergrowth; his eyes to uneasily shift. The moors began to breathe. It began to growl.

Shane's heart sank, his own breathing became heavy. Blue eyes, akin to his own, shone from behind the trees, as a large paw emerged through the trees in to Shane's sights. Claws gripped and tore up the earth beneath, a snout appeared in what remained of the headlights. Shane backed up and prepared to run. His trembling wouldn't allow him. The snout growled, composed of… anguish. A second paw came in to Shane's view, clawing itself into the earth the same as the last.

'Oh God.'

The Beast pounced on Shane, knocking him to the floor. His head smashed the concrete as he hit the road, the blue eyes that shone were almost remorseful – until the scent from Shane's torn hand reached the Beast's sinuses. Its eyes turned to a bloodlust red. Its snout violently contorted, baring its teeth, all…human, aside from the protruding canine scalpels ready to make the first incision. Shane wanted to scream, but he couldn't. The moment he opened his mouth the Beast lunged down into his throat.

Its claws dug into Shane, piercing his chest as it tore the flesh from his neck. The Beast forced down on Shane's chest, clinging harder to his skin. Shane's ribs cracked inside of him; jagged bone sliced his insides and impaled his lungs. Shane's chest was coated in his blood, his pristine white shirt was stained red. Every motion was agony-inducing, yet he strove to free himself. Blood shot from every open wound: his chest, and his neck. Shane wished for death, unconsciousness, or anything that would end the sheer pain he was in. His pain would not cease; the Beast's claws too busy tearing open his stomach. His blood oozed. Shane was in pure agony.

Shane's wish was granted, as his eyesight became faint as he lost his grip on the world.

*

A late October mist began to settle across the moors, seizing the landscape as the full moon, glorious and radiant, rose from in between the trees bare of foliage out in the horizon.

The fireflies danced, basking in the late-night, autumn air. They formed constellations in the thickening fog. There were no words carried along the breeze, not a sound – only winter's looming chill.

Tranquillity did not last – it never could.

Shane, began to stir. His eyes flickering beneath their lids and his head shook in rejection.

His wounds healed, his skin zipping back into place like a jacket. Bones snapped throughout his body. Shane's limbs broke simultaneously and elongated. His nose projected on his face forming a snout, and his canines sharpened in to fangs. His ears now took refuge atop his head with arrogant erection. His nails sharpened into murderous claws. Hair sprouted across his once damaged body, spreading over every inch of it. The heavy gasps that plagued him were now a deep growling whine.

Shane's eyelids split open. His ocean-blue eyes glared at the radiant moon; a familiar fear consumed them.

Rising from his pool of blood, the scent of iron clung to him. The aroma brought on a ferocious hunger.

A howl erupted. It echoed throughout the forest. An unkindness of ravens fled.

Samuel Stanford

Snowkissed

'Don't you touch her!' A deep voice above me sounded, followed by quick footsteps. I tried opening my eyes from where I lay on the floor, but I couldn't. I was too weak from trying to defend myself.

'Juliet!' I knew it was him; somehow. I tried to open my eyes again but all I could see were blurred shadows dancing across my vision. 'Stay away from her!' A cold wind swept through the area and I knew for sure it was him. It was icy; too icy. I shivered involuntarily and a sudden silence crept into the room.

'Jules?' His voice was softer now, closer, and I whimpered in pain. 'It's alright. Hold on now, it's going to be okay,' he murmured, just before everything went black…

My name is Juliet Charlotte Adams and this is how I fell in love.

*

He felt as though he had been wandering the earth for thousands of years; and if he was being honest he probably had. Though he'd stopped counting after the first thousand. He'd not exactly been given much information other than the ultimately significant bit; that he had to find it. He had to be the one to find the weapon that could either make or break the earth.

But no one had given him any indication as to what or who it might be. He'd only been told that he would know when he saw it; the most cliché of responses in his opinion. So he wandered. He wandered amongst people as though he was one of them; living a normal, everyday life to a certain extent. But he had to keep up with the changing times and keep up with the differing societies he encountered all around the world. Sometimes though, he just wanted to get away.

It was times like this where he'd disappear from the sights of humans around him. Granted he didn't just pop out of existence; he'd learnt that humans have no tolerance for surprises of that magnitude. But it wasn't as though he did that anyway; he just removed himself from their spectrum of sight when he wanted some time to himself – which lately seemed to be the majority of the time.

That is how he found himself wandering aimlessly through a steady trickle of human beings, who were browsing through the shop windows of the little cobbled street. He wasn't visible to a single person as he watched them explore the older parts of the city. That was when an odd movement at the end of the narrow street caught the corner of his eye and he turned to see a flash of black disappearing down the other side of the path, weaving between those still absorbed in window shopping. Curious, he followed at a cautious distance.

He paused briefly, standing on the side of the cobbled street as he searched ahead of him for the shadow of black that had caught his eye. What he didn't expect to see however, was a female stood 50 yards ahead of him; and looking right back at him.

But it wasn't the blue leather jacket or the piercing bottle green eyes that sent a chill down his body. No. It was the way a wicked smirk crept across her face as she made eye contact with him. He was told no one should be able to see him and there she was, staring right back.

He caught a mischievous glint in her eye, before she turned back around and disappeared from his sight once more. Her smirk unsettled him as he tried in vain to find her again among the masses. It certainly looked as though she could see him; but just the thought of the possibility she had seen him, would alone drive him mad for the rest of the day.

He couldn't be sure of what he'd seen, but he did spend the rest of the day wondering as he hopelessly tried seeking her out.

Gemma Strydom

The Seal Woman

She sat on the dune by the shore, knees pulled up to her chest and toes buried deep into the warm sand. Her children play nearby, one builds a sandcastle with great care, the other knocks them down moments after. She pays no attention; instead staring ahead at the waves. Where she sits is just close enough – she can feel the sea breeze blow her hair back and hear the chirps of seagulls on the cliffs, but the spray of the summer waves is still just out of reach. Within her hands she clutches a grey material; soft, dry, it squeaks beneath her fingers like rubber. It's cool to the touch, but her heart flutters in her chest as she traces the creases with her fingertips. She'd found it in the garden buried beneath the roots of the apple tree, dug up one day by her loyal terrier. She'd never felt happiness like it – not on her wedding day, not when her kids were born, never.

She stands, brushing the sand from herself, and steps further onto the beach. The children notice as she passes. She pauses at their tiny voices:

'Mummy?'

'Where are you going?'

The pull became too much, and she began to move again. She was running now, skipping over the sand with a huge grin across her face. The closer she got to the ocean the more the hole in her heart shrunk. She kicked off her shoes as she reached the wet sand; the water welcomed her with an ice-cold hug. The sensation of the sand beneath her toes and the current against her ankles lifted every weight from her shoulders. Movement caught her eye; two seals bobbing in the distance, waiting for her. She lingered in the shallows for a while, the waves lapping against her knees and pulling the trailing grey rubber to and fro. Closing her eyes, she raised her face towards the sun. She'd loved to sunbathe on the beaches as a pup, careless and free. Now, she vowed never to leave the waves.

She waded further – the crashing waves drowning out the screams of her children – embracing the pull by stripping off the simple dress she wore, letting the wind take it. Once the water lapped her waist and the waiting seals drifted close enough to touch, she took the material in two hands and wrapped the smooth skin around her human legs. Warmth spread through her body, fusing human with seal. Soon she was buoyant, drifting as her legs became one. Bones rearranged, muscles growing and shrinking, but it wasn't painful. Then, as if all at once, she was whole again.

She was home.

Megan Tait-Davies

The Swan

In my house, we were quiet.

That wasn't a good thing. I don't mean we were calm or we were all the types who sat with our heads in books. I mean we didn't talk. Not really. Not about anything that mattered.

And when I say we, I mean they. In our house, they were quiet. I was never good at being quiet, not like they were. Mum says I was born with a pair of lungs on me, screaming fit to bring half the ward running to see what had happened at the slightest inconvenience. She'd say it like it was meant to be fond but the smile she had when she talked about it never quite reached her eyes.

It was my brother who taught me to be quiet. He was older than me. Smarter. He was the planned-for baby. He understood the rules.

It took me a long time to learn that there were two types of not-talking. There was the normal kind of not-talking. This was where everything was fine. We'd sit for hours, all watching the TV and not-talking. Or making dinner and not-talking. Or talking about things like the weather and what was on TV that evening, swerving deftly around any controversial topic. This kind of not-talking was fine. There was the kind of not-talking where, if you interrupted it by singing silly songs from school or asking questions, you'd get a frown and a quiet reminder that good girls weren't loud.

It was the other kind of not-talking that was the problem for me. The kind of not-talking where you're not-talking about something.

When I was little, I knew it was that kind of not-talking because my brother would come and get me before I could yell or tell a joke or do something else to really upset someone. On the kind of days when we were not-talking about something, he'd take me out into the garden or up into his room and he'd tell me stories.

His favourite story, the one he told me time and again, was a fairytale. A story about seven brothers turned into swans who were saved by their dutiful sister who took a vow of silence and knit them each a shirt from brambles.

My favourite stories were ones where things blew up.

As I got older, I got better at telling the difference between the two kinds of not-talking. When we were not-talking about something, mum would hold her back straighter and stare straight ahead. Dad would avoid eye contact at all cost and cough more, like he wanted to cross the silence somehow but wasn't sure how to. Like there was some deficit in him. The very air of the house seemed to change. It became thin, making noises seem further away and spaces colder. The clanging of a pot in the kitchen might as well be in another country, when we weren't talking about something.

As we got older, I got better at noticing when we weren't talking about something, but I never quite got it perfect.

That's why, when I was twelve, I said into the not-talking about something, 'Was that your boyfriend we caught you kissing, Danny?'

The thing with the not-talking about something was it was delicate, and if you smashed it, you did so at your own peril.

There was a lot of yelling that night. A lot of slamming of doors. For a while I was right there in it, waving my arms and stamping my feet until I was sent to my room. I lay on the floor, pressing my ear to the thin pink carpet and listening, trying to make out the words below. I thought how unfair it was that people were finally talking and I'd been sent away.

The next morning I asked mum where Danny was. She turned away. Dad ruffled his newspaper.

I snuck into Danny's room that afternoon. It took me too long to realise things were gone. Some clothes. His favourite book. The trophy he won when he left primary school for having the best test results in his year.

I realised, then, that maybe breaking the not-talking about something had been the wrong thing to do.

I went back to my room. I lay on the floor again, pressing my cheek to the carpet like I could call the shouting back by listening for it, but the floorboards were silent. I curled up under my bed and thought about the sister whose brothers turned into swans.

I took my own vow of silence that day: ten years old, lost and alone. I decided that if I couldn't tell the difference, it was better to just never talk at all.

It was hard at first, of course. The words bubbled up in me all the time, straining to come out and I'd never been good at holding them in, pushing them down. I took another page from my fairy-tale and asked Mum to teach me how to knit. She was happy to and from then, whenever I'd feel the need to talk, to shout, build up in my throat, I'd grab my knitting. I'd run the yarn through my finger and push all the anger and confusion into the stitch. Lock it up and hide it away in the fabric.

It took years before I was good enough to make a shirt. I made scarves. I made hats. I made a dishcloth in nice colours for mum's birthday. I made a blanket for my cousin's baby.

Sometimes I thought I saw Danny, when we were in town. Once I thought he had a moustache. Once I thought he was with another man, that they were laughing together.

I found the jumper pattern in a charity shop. It involved complex cabling, perfect for hiding angry words in. I asked for the yarn for Christmas. Mum was happy to get me it. She liked that I knit. She'd smile and say things like, 'this one might not be the smartest but she's hard working and good with her hands'.

It took nearly a year to finish the jumper, in between GCSEs. It's done now, though. It's all done. Jumper and school and everything. I've packed it away in a bag under by bed with my favourite clothes, a teddy from when I was little that I wouldn't want to lose. I haven't packed my knitting needles; I don't need them anymore.

My jumper is done, my curse is lifted. Tonight, I'm going to ask again about Danny and this time, when we don't talk about it, I'm going to scream.

E. L. Thompson

The Flowers That Frighten Me

Standing tall and stiff and still,
Like soldiers in a row,
The red and purple tulips,
In straight long lines do grow.

Very proud and grand they look,
I'm sure they've never played.
If I was a fairy small
Of them I'd be afraid.

But fairies do not seem to think
Of minding them a bit!
They shake the stalks and climb up them,
And in the flowers sit.

They slide along the leaves,
Which must be very tough,
Those bad fairies pull them so,
Oh, they can be rough!

And then I'm frightened just in case
Those cross tulips might
Do something rather dreadful
To pay them back one night.

For the tulips talk at dusk
If the fairies are not there.
I listened once and heard them.
It gave me quite a scare!

And everyone was whispering,
Heads nodding up and down.
They looked as if they had real faces
And every face wore a frown.

And they planned such dreadful things,
And said they'd do them too!
I'm frightened for the fairies,
In case, one day, they do.

Holly Whitford

The Midnight Ride with the Púca

A colt waits at the edge of the forest, snorting vapor into the icy winter night. Anger oozes from his coat like steam, nostrils flaring towards the poorly lit farmhouse. He rises, shakes out his mane and rattles the steel chains that cling about his neck and ankles.

The family of five inside can hear him, they know he is waiting. Father fetches his dagger from the large oak dresser. His voice trembles as he ushers them all back to their beds, ordering them to pull their blankets over their heads and cover their ears.

He drums the grass with his hooves, gauging deep wounds into the earth.

'It is time for you to ride. It is time for you to settle your debt.'

The sound radiates through the earth, a bass and soprano duet, conflicting. Unsettled yet soothed, the children lower their blankets and listen. They have been warned, since birth, never to cross a Púca.

He rears up, releasing a braying laugh, all four limbs retract. His body shifts towards a human shape, except the ears which remain unchanged. He retains the thick black fur which spreads across his new palms and fingers as he reaches out towards the house. The watchful eyes that crouch behind the windowsill do not notice the empty beds of their children, and once the small hands close around his fingers, they become his.

Jess Whittall

The Recorder

Eric had always felt a strong desire for preservation. This was quite a useful desire, as he also had an ongoing tendency to lose things. A file at the bottom of his wardrobe held hundreds of receipts, at least half of which were for replacement keys, or phones. The receipts suggested that they be retained for his records, and so they were. His family mocked him for this near-daily. 'What sort of teenager collects useless scraps of paper?'

He was sure that one day soon those records would prove necessary. If he was ever to be dragged into a police station and asked his whereabouts on the 12th of September 2009, he would simply retrieve his file from the bottom of the wardrobe and pull out the plastic wallet marked '2009'. Then from that he would pull out a smaller plastic wallet marked 'September'. From the index cards inside he would be able to locate every single receipt from the 12th.

The first of these would be a bus ticket. That day he had caught the bus from the stop nearest to his house, less than 20 metres away, between 8am and 9am. He had ridden into town from the often-forgotten outskirts where his family was living at the time. He remembers that they were often-forgotten, because there was a delay for the bus almost every day – the private companies in charge of getting the busses to run on time overlooked the citizens of the outskirts. Direct Travel sent out their busses only when it was convenient. It was almost impossible for Eric's neighbours to hold down decent jobs due to frequent tardiness. This meant that there was not a lot of money in the outskirts, which, in turn, meant that there were very few shops in the outskirts. This meant that there were fewer jobs in the outskirts, and most of the residents had to catch the late busses into the surrounding towns for interviews that would be over before they arrived. Perhaps the interviewer would overlook the lateness if they could guarantee it wouldn't continue to be an issue. Of course, it would, but the busses were the only option for most of Eric's neighbours. They had never kept one job long enough to secure a loan for a car or to establish any savings that wouldn't be devoured by the ensuing months of unemployment. The only people that had their own cars with which to drive into the towns and cities for stable employment were the ones who had arrived with their cars and their stable employment in search of lower property prices. For them, this had the handy benefit of allowing them to set more money aside for retirement.

From the bus, Eric had walked a short while through town. The air was beginning to cool, and his shabby coat was not quite enough to stop a chill running through his slim body. He stopped at a family run café for a cup of burnt coffee and a greasy bacon sandwich. They looked at him funny when he asked for a receipt. The woman with grey hair pulled tightly back poured the coffee, smiled, and asked what he was doing in town. He replied that he had just received his final payslip from the chain restaurant down the street. His mother's birthday was in a few days, so he needed to buy her a present. The woman suggested a box of chocolates.

'It's not much, like, but when me weans give me a box of chocolate with a little card what they wrote I feel like the best mam in the whole country.'

He asked why she didn't say the world. She replied that she wasn't that cocky. Eric finished his coffee, wiped the remnants away from his pale lips. He left the café and took a short walk down to the restaurant in which he had used to work, trying to smooth his unruly black hair before he went inside. He asked to see Kevin, who had until recently been his manager. In the office he had explained his situation and politely requested to exchange the cheque he had been given for cash. Kevin explained that that wasn't something he could do. He would have loved to be able to help – after all, Eric had been an ideal employee when he could manage to make it on time – but it just wasn't possible. Eric had thanked him anyway and told him that he would head straight to the bank to deposit the cheque. With a bit of luck, it might clear before his share of the bills needed to be paid. On the way out, Eric spotted the till temporarily abandoned, a rare opportunity. He slipped behind the counter, avoiding the surveillance cameras monitoring the patrons every move. He punched in the supervisory code. The drawer sprang open easily. He only took what he was sure wouldn't be noticed until Friday when the cash would be counted. It totalled less than £150, but that would cover him and his family for a couple of weeks at least. He would tell them not to worry about where the money had come from, that it was just a little extra in his wages as a parting gift. His family would worry about where the money had come from regardless, knowing that he had parted ways from the restaurant on less than good terms despite the overt friendliness of the manager. They wouldn't question him about it, knowing all too well that when a youngster from their area comes into a little extra money, suspicious questions can lead to official questions which can lead to courtrooms and forking out money that they didn't have for a suit that nobody wanted to buy.

The next receipt that he pulled out would show that he had indeed headed to the bank, arriving there just 10 minutes after he set off. It was slightly less than a 10-minute walk, but who's to say he didn't stop to chat to a friend on the way? The receipts tell the hypothetical officer that he had deposited a cheque for £405.67 into his bank account, bring the total balance up to just above 0, before overdraft charges and interest payments took it back into negative figures. The bank was just across the road from the supermarket, a road which he crossed in a hurry. He had walked into the supermarket and stood still on the flat escalators that took him up from the car park to the produce aisle. He always enjoyed the feeling of motionlessness as you reached your destination. It was the same feeling he got sitting perfectly still in a train seat, watching the houses speed off behind him, leaving nothing in their wake. No receipts. No records. Without a single step he reached the supermarket floor, shooting nervous glances around him. The security guard smiled. Eric walked briskly into the store, headed for the confectionary aisle. The unbreakable gaze of the cameras followed his path, silently observing every step from entrance to exit.

Scott Winsbury

Waiting

Your ink and paper pink entrap me now;
Biro bars, blind scrivening to indict.
What moral failures pennings do allow.
What need for such high powers recondite?
Safety mine and safety yours. Such old lies.
Tattoo my crimes and wipe away my will;
You carve your name on stones of my demise,
Form barriers and vows to keep me still.
Is the pen so mighty? Papers binding?
Tissue walls and pigment-stained deceptions.
Other ways exist to help unwinding –
Tolerate, don't quarter me in sections.
Revolt! Fuck you all! See your sentence gored!
Wounded words, skewered on my lettered sword.

David Yeomans

Bloodjack

Dancing orange fag ends
Stirred the inky treacle air
Buzzing silhouettes of bonny lads and glowing girls
Orbited each other like teacups
The babbles of vibrant conversationalists
Gushed up and washed away all the laughing bairns
As if life was a pipe running under the Earth
And we burst it
On that dying night

Last stands were made
On a podium at the back of the dancefloor
Desperados on the end of each arm
Up in the air
Screaming and waving to Heaven
With the rest of the committed crowd
You'd hoped some stranger who'd always been looking for you
Would spot you at long last
On that dying night

I'll never forget twisting through the throng to find you
Pissed to bits and shimmering with mischief
Spanking some radge packet with an inflatable sex doll taped to his back
A Burger King crown cocked on your head
You seized me with a hand slapped round the back of my neck
Pulled your sweaty forehead to mine
'I'm taking off mate I'm going to see the world!'
You cried
On that dying night

From our perch we watched a boy being slogged
We shook our heads and said 'summat should be done about that'
This shaking man bared his teeth like a pissed off dog
As if the walls were closing in to prick and poke his pride
He belted out rude heat that stunk like a grotesque birth

Frank fists on wet wood
There wasn't a spot of blood left in that poor cunt's gob
It was all over us
On that dying night

We were all flushed out onto the road outside
And we shambled together into the callous morning light
Lost children in a motherless market
Coming down like pigeons caught in murder holes
Falling out gently like gnarly hair from a rotting scalp
And as they swirled away down the scaly drain
You said goodbye to the ones you left behind
One last time
On that dying night

The boards are up and the shops are shut
The dancefloor sank under the tarry black pavement
Birthday parties and weekend bus trips
Became choral myths and lies whispered in hollow ruins
Haggard auld punters shuffle about in quiet pubs
And foggy smiles break their stony faces
When dead men tell tall tales
Of who they were
On that dying night

I watched a centipede burrow limbs flailing into your breaking back
And you popped and bubbled like a cluster of hatching eggs
Ten thousand stamping feet rattled up the gaping street
As you scrabbled away into the shade of the ancient walls
Sneering letters flittered down from the sun in silent confetti
Forming unfriendly complex words from classrooms locked and guarded
They stotted off your skull and buckled and humped your spine
And now you are an aching arch straddled by the mossy viaduct
On a scorching heartless day

Tom Young

Acknowledgements

Thank you to all the writers, artists and designers who submitted their work for consideration for this anthology. Each of the pieces offers an insight into their immense creativity, and we hope to see more from them all in the future. We would also like to thank everyone involved in the publication of the Beyond the Walls 2018 anthology. Their dedication is what made this all possible.

The Editorial Team 1 2018

Aimee Donnell; Georgia Fenwick; Elle Hartley Smith; Jennifer Keighley; Alice Leon; John Liddle; Benjamin Shaw; Jackson Smith; Megan Tait-Davies; Silje Tunes Huse; Paul Whelan; Jess Whittall; Anneke Wind

The Editorial Team 2 2018

Elizabeth Bell; Stacy Curry; Elsie Franklin; Georgia Hackman; Natasha Hindmarsh; Emily Holmes; Georgina Kerr; Thomas Markham; Harry Mitchell; Charles Prudames; James Rance; Sarah Ratcliffe; Sophie Swainson

Thank you to those who promoted and publicised the anthology:

The Promotions Team 2018

Charlotte Bennett; Victoria Booth; Izi Dewhurst; Rosalind Griffiths; Caitlain Horan; Samuel Jacques; Alex McGowan; Bradley Patching; Charlie Plumb; Amba Smith; Tia Welsh; Jessica Wright

Thank you to those who organised and managed the launch of the anthology:

The Events Team 2018

Ben Ambrazaitis; Lucinda Bennett; Elizabeth Fitzgerald; Kate Hewett; Elle Hurst; Grace Morris; Abbi Peace; Imogen Peniston; Georgia Ritson; Jessica Shabi; Niamh Stamper; Gabriel Williamson

We are very grateful to BA (Hons) Graphic Design student Hannah Ford for designing the cover for the anthology.

Valley Press have been a vital asset to the production of Beyond the Walls 2018 and we are extremely appreciative of Jamie McGarry and Vanessa Simmons for sharing their professional knowledge and providing us with the ability to share our writing with the world. We thank Valley Press authors Nora Chassler and Nigel Forde for reading at the event.

We thank YSJ alumna and novelist Nuala Ellwood for officially launching our anthology.

Finally, we would like to thank Dr Kimberly Campanello for her extensive insight, phenomenal leadership and persistence in ensuring work of the highest standards. The Publishing, Production and Performance module on the BA (Hons) Creative Writing course has provided each student with invaluable knowledge and experience of the publishing sector.